HOMOSEXUALITY & THE CATHOLIC CHURCH

Clear Answers to Difficult Questions

Fr. John F. Harvey, O.S.F.S.

Foreword by
Most Reverend Raymond L. Burke, D.D., J.C.D.,
Archbishop of St. Louis

Introduction by
Fr. Benedict Groeschel, C.F.R., Ph.D.

ASCENSION PRESS

West Chester, Pennsylvania

Nihil obstat: Rev. J. Brian Bransfield, S.T.D.
             Censor Librorum
             October 11, 2007

Imprimatur: +Justin Cardinal Rigali
             Archbishop of Philadelphia
             October 13, 2007

Ascension Press
Post Office Box 1990
West Chester, PA 19380
Orders: 1-800-376-0520
www.AscensionPress.com

Cover design: Kinsey Caruth

Printed in the United States of America
07 08 09 10 11 7 6 5 4 3 2 1

ISBN: 978-1-932927-62-7

CONTENTS

ACKNOWLEDGMENTS

I owe a debt of thanks to Edward Cardinal Egan, Archbishop of New York, for his support in allowing me to take time off from my work in New York to write another book on homosexual questions; to the Very Reverend Joseph Morrissey, O.S.F.S., Provincial of the Wilmington-Philadelphia Province of the Oblates of St. Francis de Sales, who granted me permission to live at Ave Maria University while counseling college men in the process of discerning a vocation to the Catholic priesthood; to Mr. Thomas Monaghan, Chancellor of Ave Maria University, for the gift of a fellowship for the purpose of writing this book; to Father Benedict Groeschel, C.F.R., for writing the introduction; to Father Michael Beers, the superior of the pre-theologate program; to Ann Lukomski, who was my secretary in putting this book together; to Dan Hilker, who helped edit the original version of the manuscript; to Tina and Frank at the Courage office for sent documents; to the acting director of Courage, Father James Lloyd, C.S.P.; and to all others who have helped me, particularly the librarians of Ave Maria University.

I also thank the following persons and organizations for permission to reprint material:

- Evergreen International and its executive director, David Pruden; Exodus International and its president, Alan Chambers; Homosexuals Anonymous; IHF (Jews Offering New Alternatives to Homosexuality) and its director, Arthur Goldberg; PFOX (Parents and Friends of Ex-Gays and Gays) and its CEO, Regina Griggs — for use of materials from their respective websites.

- NARTH (National Association for Research and Therapy of Homosexuality) for permission to reprint excerpts from the summary of Linda Nicolosi and Roy Waller of "Spitzer Study Just Published Evidence Found in Effectiveness of Reorientation Therapy," *NARTH Bulletin*, vol. 12, no. 3 (Dec. 2003), pp. 1-2; also for being a channel of references for those working with people of same-sex attraction.

- PATH (Positive Alternatives to Homosexuality) for the existence of PATH, which makes it easy for members to cooperate with each other and for the use of the materials used from different members.

- Catholic Medical Association for use of my article published in the May 1993 issue of the *Linacre Quarterly* entitled "The Pastoral Problem of Masturbation."

- Maggie Gallagher and Joshua Baker for their contribution from the social sciences in defense of the rights of the child and of the institution of traditional marriage in the best interests of the child, in chapter 4.

- Professor Gerard Bradley for his argument against gay "marriage" in chapter 4, and for his article, "The Court Will Amend the Constitution If Congress Doesn't," *National Review Online*, April 14, 2005.

- Kenneth D. Whitehead for his article, "Why Same-Sex Marriage Is a Bad Idea," *Catholic World Report*, August-September 2004, pp. 56-57.

- Zenit Vatican News Service for permission to use two interviews with Zenit: "Recognizing and Treating Same-Sex Attractions in Children," November 16, 2003 and "Source of Same-Sex Attractions in Children," January 24, 2004.

- Susan Brinkmann of the *Catholic Standard & Times* of Philadelphia who interviewed Vera concerning her reparational group.

- Fr. James Knapp, S. J., for the gift of an annotated bibliography.

FOREWORD

Some time ago, at the conclusion of a reception following the conferral of the sacrament of Confirmation, a mother approached me and asked whether she could speak with me. She began by saying that, while she did not want to offend me, she disagreed with a column I had written in the archdiocesan newspaper. The column was written at the time that the citizens of Missouri were preparing to vote on a referendum to amend the state constitution to define marriage as the union of one man and one woman—that is, to ban what has become popularly known as "same-sex marriage" or "gay marriage."

This well-spoken mother told me that she was offended because my article implied that her daughter was evil. She went on to explain that her daughter, who is in her early twenties, had graduated from a private Catholic high school with highest honors and with many awards. She has been active in a same-sex relationship for some time. With great emotion, the mother declared her love for her daughter, which, according to her way of thinking, requires acceptance and support of her daughter's same-sex relationship, including welcoming her daughter and her same-sex partner into the family home.

I explained to the mother that I have never thought nor written that persons suffering from same-sex attraction are evil. I went on to summarize what I had written in the column to which she referred, namely, that same-sex attraction itself is disordered—that is, contrary to God's plan for us as male and female; that homosexual acts are intrinsically evil; and that persons with same-sex attraction are our brothers and sisters, whom we are to respect and love. The mother continued to insist that she loves her daughter and, therefore, will support her in her same-sex relationship.

The conversation in question reminded me of several pastoral situations in which I have found a parent struggling painfully with the homosexual activity of a child. The emotion of the situation can understandably cloud one's judgment. Whereas in the past, such emotion may have led parents to reject a child suffering with the homosexual condition or to pretend that the condition did not exist, today there is a tendency for parents to believe that tolerance requires them to accept the homosexual activity of their child and even permit it in the family home.

Given the strong public rhetoric favoring the acceptance of same-sex attraction and homosexual activity as an alternative form of human sexuality, the very presentation of the Catholic Church's perennial teaching on the matter is considered, at best, failing in pastoral sensitivity; at worst, hateful toward persons who struggle with same-sex attraction. The theological truth is seen to be somehow antithetical to the pastoral or loving response required. For that reason, Catholic faithful, including the clergy, can become hesitant to present and clearly uphold the Church's teaching on homosexual inclinations and activity. At the same time, the persistent public message about homosexuality—in the absence of a consistent presentation of the Church's teaching—can easily lead the Catholic faithful into confused and even erroneous thinking on the matter.

As at no other time, our society and culture needs to hear the voice of the Church, teaching the divine natural moral law, which safeguards the common good and, therefore, the good of each individual. There can be no pastorally sensitive or loving approach which is not fully informed by and consistent with the teaching of the Church. What is needed is the conviction that the truth communicated with love is the fullest expression of our love and compassion toward every brother and sister.

For that reason, I thank God for Father John F. Harvey, O.S.F.S., and his many decades of dedicated priestly service on behalf of persons who suffer with same-sex attraction. Father Harvey's pastoral care of the faithful who, in some way, are dealing with the homosexual condition is founded on a profound and ongoing study of the condition itself and of the Church's teaching in the matter. Father Harvey's highly qualified study and compassionate pastoral care have led him to establish two support groups for persons desiring to live the truth of the Church's teaching regarding homosexuality and homosexual acts. The genius of the support groups is the recognition that homosexuality is not the identity of the person who struggles with same-sex attraction. The identity of the person is, rather, that of a child of God called to the virtue of chastity, to the way of chaste love of neighbor. Recognizing the true identity of the person, the support groups help everyone to grow in the freedom which comes from being true to who we are.

The first support group is called Courage. It is for those who suffer from same-sex attraction and want to receive support and to give support in practicing the virtue of chastity. The second is called Encourage. It is for parents and siblings of persons suffering from same-sex attraction who want to receive support and give support in authentic love of sons, daughters, brothers, and sisters who are affected by the homosexual condition. From my pastoral experience, I know how profoundly helpful both support groups have been for their members. It is my hope that, one day, there will be chapters of Courage and Encourage readily available to all who seek to know the truth about homosexuality and to live that truth with love. In my conversation with the mother after the Confirmation ceremony, I urged her to have contact with the local chapter of Encourage. I hope that she did.

Father Harvey's long and distinguished experience in the pastoral care of persons affected by the homosexual condition has already borne fruit in two books. *The Homosexual Person*, published in 1987, and *The Truth about Homosexuality*, published in 1996, have been of inestimable assistance to all who want to understand homosexuality and respond in a Christ-like manner to brothers and sisters who struggle with same-sex attraction. Father Harvey has also edited, with Professor Gerard V. Bradley of the University of Notre Dame, a third book, *Same Sex Attraction: A Parent's Guide*, published in 2003. As the title indicates, it is especially directed to parents whose children struggle with the homosexual condition.

It is an honor for me to present to you Father Harvey's latest work, *Homosexuality & the Catholic Church*. This question-and-answer book will help you gain a deeper appreciation of the Church's teachings on homosexuality and the ever more pressing question of same-sex "marriage," as well as the importance of support groups such as Courage and Encourage in helping those with same-sex attraction live chaste lives. In these pages, Father Harvey helps us all to think more clearly and to act more rightly and lovingly in responding to our brothers and sisters with same-sex attraction, especially those who wrongly desire to enter a kind of "marriage," which, in fact, is no marriage at all and a contradiction of the nature of marriage.

I thank Father Harvey for yet one more important contribution to the authentic pastoral care of persons affected by homosexuality. I pray that God will continue to bless abundantly Father Harvey and all the members of Courage and Encourage.

I conclude with the story of a more recent pastoral encounter. Not long ago, I celebrated the ordination of permanent deacons for the service of the archdiocese. At the conclusion of the Mass of Ordination, I remained in the narthex of the Cathedral Basilica of Saint Louis to greet the faithful. As I was returning to the sacristy, a young man came across the aisle to greet me. He was beaming with joy. He shook my hand and said these simple words: "Thank you for Courage." He then briefly told me how participation in Courage has transformed his life. The joy and peace radiating from his face were a testimonial to the truth of his words. I have had similar experiences on other occasions.

Through the work of Courage and Encourage, may many more men and women who struggle with same-sex attraction know the joy and peace of a chaste life in Christ. May this latest fruit of Father John Harvey's study and pastoral work help us all to uphold, in word and in deed, chaste love and the integrity of the married life.

—Most Reverend Raymond L. Burke
Archbishop of St. Louis
July 22, 2007
Memorial of Saint Mary Magdalene

PREFACE

In my two previous books, *The Homosexual Person* (Ignatius Press, 1987) and *The Truth about Homosexuality* (Ignatius Press, 1996), I cover many aspects of homosexuality. In *The Homosexual Person*, with the help of Fr. Jeffrey Keefe, O.F.M. Conv., a clinical psychologist, I consider the psychological and physical aspects of homosexuality, the morality of homosexual acts, and the need for a spiritual support system for Catholics who truly desire to lead a chaste life in accord with Catholic doctrine. The remainder of the volume is devoted to a variety of pastoral problems, as well as psychological insights from Elizabeth Moberly and Gerard van den Aardweg concerning the origins and treatment of homosexual behavior. In *The Truth about Homosexuality*, I discuss at length various controversies in the field: Father Jeffrey Keefe, again, reflects on the various theories about the origins of this condition; I review the literature concerning the possibility of recovering one's natural heterosexual inclinations; and distinguished therapists in the Catholic tradition, Drs. Maria Valdes and Richard Fitzgibbons, share their wisdom with our readers.

Following the publication of these two works, Gerard Bradley, Professor of Law at the University of Notre Dame, in 1998 joined me in the preparation of an anthology of readings for members of Encourage, a support group which grew out of Courage, for parents and relatives of persons with same-sex attraction who are heartbroken over their son's or daughter's refusal to live by the teaching of the Church. Such persons need spiritual support even as their children do. Scholars in psychological and clinical research, theologians in Scripture, moral theology, and canon law, as well as civil law scholars, Catholic laity, cardinals, and a Protestant pastoral leader all provide insight and encouragement for parents who need spiritual support in attaining active resignation to God's mysterious permissive will. This anthology is entitled *Same Sex Attraction: A Parent's Guide* and was published by St. Augustine's Press in 2003.

Over the past few years, I have felt the need for another book. So much has happened since *The Truth about Homosexuality* was published in 1996: the gay movement has grown stronger throughout the world; the general public has accepted uncritically the media's advocacy of same-sex unions as an acceptable alternative to traditional marriage; and many heterosexual people have come to believe that people with same-sex attraction (SSA) are not able to be chaste—indeed, many persons with SSA also believe that they are not able to be chaste, and act accordingly.

There are two purposes in writing this book: the first is to provide an overview of some basic concepts involved in same-sex attraction and to help readers understand how persons with same-sex attractions can learn to live chastely; and the second is to provide an authentic Catholic perspective on the topic of same-sex unions and gay "marriage." It is necessary to provide the individual with spiritual direction and a regular program, the purpose of which would be to help individuals learn how to be chaste. As we developed such a program (i.e., Courage), we began to speak with parents of persons with SSA and realized that they too needed help, just like the spouse of an alcoholic.

In later chapters, I describe the nature and goals of both Courage and Encourage, and explain the value of the Twelve Steps in helping persons with same-sex attraction to live chaste lives. I also include a detailed chapter on spiritual direction and present a discussion of the relationship of Courage to other organizations that seek to help persons with unwanted same-sex attractions, as well as a listing of Catholic groups who are not in full agreement with the authentic teaching of the Church.

—Fr. John F. Harvey, O.S.F.S.
Director, Courage

INTRODUCTION

Twenty years ago, I was invited by Father John Harvey to write an introduction for his book *The Homosexual Person*. This work really marked the success of his efforts during a thirty-year period to offer pastoral assistance to Catholics with a homosexual inclination who were seeking to lead chaste lives. Several years before the book was published, Terence Cardinal Cooke, Archbishop of New York, had asked me to try to find a way to help homosexually oriented Catholics lead a chaste life. As soon as he spoke to me, I thought of Father Harvey's outstanding work in this area over the years, for which he had received relatively little recognition.

From the saintly Cardinal's suggestion came the Courage movement, which Father Harvey began shortly thereafter. The Archdiocese of New York initially supported the work of Courage, and the first group was founded in Manhattan. Subsequently, the movement grew, as we see in the pages that follow, and became an international organization in the English-speaking world. The Courage and Encourage movements have assisted innumerable people in their own lives and in the lives of those dear to them.

When Father Harvey began his work with homosexually oriented people nearly fifty years ago in Pennsylvania, there was practically no recognition of the needs of those seeking to lead a chaste life. Homosexual orientation was hardly ever spoken about. It was an act of divine providence that Father Harvey came along and put Catholic efforts on an equal footing with those made by a number of evangelical Protestant associations. In time large numbers of priests, parents, and other interested friends have joined Courage members in offering a Christian and morally acceptable alternative to the so-called gay scene.

Although other organizations made up of Catholics seek to assist people with same-sex attraction, Courage is clearly and unequivocally the one that tries to follow the teachings of the Gospel, the New Testament, and Church Tradition. Gradually, the hierarchy and the Church have extended to the Courage movement some of the support it so obviously deserves.

At the present moment some new developments and challenges have come along, which Father Harvey has tried to address in this volume. The most obvious one is the proposal of so-called same-sex marriage, which would unquestionably undermine the institution of marriage, already under attack in the United States and many other Western countries. Efforts to give legal acceptance to same-sex unions and place them on a par with the family bring with them a tremendous threat to the family. Unfortunately, those who propose same-sex "marriages" often fail to recognize the damage they will inadvertently but inevitably cause to family life. Also the public acceptance of homosexual inclinations in the entertainment and other media often exposes young people to homosexual attractions. One of the purposes of a well-organized culture is to guide children toward heterosexual orientation, on which the future of society depends.

This book explores many of the implications of the general movement toward having homosexual relations accepted as part of life, as an arrangement equivalent to marriage. One of my concerns is that this movement may backfire, and the progress already made to protect homosexually oriented people from the deprivation of their rights and from public harassment may be lost. Some genuine progress has been made to give people rightful protection. If the proponents of so-called gay rights push the envelope too far, it may very well lead to a negative reaction across the board. Already in recent elections there seems to be an observable and negative trend developing. Those familiar with the sociology and psychology of political trends will realize that these changes can take place with startling rapidity.

In the midst of this chaos, Courage and a number of evangelical Protestant movements are calling people to a chaste Christian life. Some even invite people to reverse their orientation so that they can enter into marriage. Several faith-centered therapeutic programs have had remarkable success in achieving this.

It is very interesting that some who were involved in removing the homosexual diagnosis from the *Diagnostic and Statistical Manual (DSM)* of the American Psychiatric Association have subsequently changed their opinion on the clinical aspects of homosexual orientation and admitted this publicly. They have accepted the fact that with strong religious motivation it is quite possible to reverse the orientation so that marriage becomes for some a possibility.

The issue of same-sex "marriage" and a number of other contemporary issues related to homosexuality are taken up in this volume. The spiritual aspects of the challenge facing people with same-sex attraction—the struggle to maintain chastity and to lead a chaste life—find their way into everyone's life. And the homosexually oriented person is called to chastity just as much as anyone else. Father Harvey gives us some important observations and suggestions on leading a chaste life in the face of homosexual inclinations.

If you have the opportunity to attend a Courage conference, as I have, you will be deeply impressed not only by the whole program but also by the sincerity and prayerfulness of the individual members. Courage is truly a beautiful example of Saint Paul's words: "Where sin increased, grace abounded all the more" (Romans 5:20). If you cannot easily attend a Courage conference, reading this volume will bring you up-to-date and give you insight into a marvelous work of grace.

Although I initially contacted Father Harvey at the suggestion of Cardinal Cooke, I have not been able, with my own responsibilities, to take much of a hand in the Courage struggle. I have managed to get to a few national conferences. I want to congratulate the many priests and laypeople who have worked with Courage. I particularly salute the members of Encourage, as well as the rank and file members of Courage—those who in an outstanding way have stood against the tide of the media and at times have suffered ridicule and loneliness because of their stand for chastity. I am convinced that, in the relatively near future, Courage will reap a great harvest of souls for God and that Christ's words in the New Testament will take root in the hearts of many. Father Harvey's initial work and his brave pioneers will reap much fruit. Don't stand on the sidelines. Read this book and rejoice that the work of the Holy Spirit still continues in our confused world.

—Fr. Benedict J. Groeschel, C.F.R.
Author, *The Courage to Be Chaste*

CHAPTER 1

Homosexuality: Some Basic Questions

1. How can homosexuality be defined?

Traditionally, homosexuality (or same-sex attraction) has been described as a *persistent* and *predominant* attraction of a sexual-genital nature to persons of one's own sex. The term "persistent" is used to indicate that such erotic feelings toward someone of the same sex have persisted beyond adolescence. The term "predominant" is used to indicate that there may be a lesser degree of erotic interest in the other sex.

Dr. Gerard van den Aardweg offers another version of the traditional definition: "We shall reserve the word homosexual (homophile) here for erotic wishes directed to members of the same sex, accompanied by a reduction of erotic interests in the opposite sex."[1]

In yet another view, Dr. Elizabeth Moberly holds that a homosexual orientation "does not depend on a genetic dispositional hormonal imbalance or abnormal learning processes, but on difficulties in the parent-child relationship, especially in the early years of life."[2]

While admitting the complexity of homosexual phenomena, Moberly singles out one underlying principle: that the homosexual man or woman suffers from a deficit in his or her relationship with the parent of the same sex, and that there is a corresponding drive to make good this deficit through the medium of same-sex or homosexual relationships.

2. So persons with same-sex attraction have a "deficit" in their relationship with their same-sex parent?

Yes. The term "deficit" as used in the previous answer refers to an inadequacy due to some kind of trauma that has destroyed the natural attachment to the same-sex parent, leaving the child unfulfilled in his or her need for same-sex attachment. It does not imply any willful neglect or maltreatment of the child by the parent of the same sex.[3]

3. Is Dr. Moberly saying that homosexuality is a symptom of something else?

No, Moberly understands what is generally termed *homosexuality* to be a condition of same-sex ambivalence that is primarily a gender-identity problem rather than a sexual-genital problem. As the child represses his or her normal need for attachment to the parent of his or her own sex, the opposite drive for restoration of the attachment is strengthened. This defensive detachment, coupled with the urge for renewed attachment, results in a condition of same-sex ambivalence.[4]

4. How is Moberly's definition different from the traditional view of homosexuality?

The traditional view of homosexuality focuses on the sexual-genital desire for another person of the same sex, whereas Moberly's definition is concerned with one's ambivalence concerning gender identity. This condition exists in the person prior to, and independent of, any sexual activity. Significantly, the person's need for gender identity can (and should) be met independently of any sexual activity.[5]

5. **So the traditional view of homosexuality, which centers on sexual desire and activity, does not adequately explain its true cause?**

No, because the traditional view does not explain the empirical data concerning same-sex animosity. Homosexual persons have both *attraction to* and *hostility toward* persons of the same sex. The media refers to "same-sex love" (meaning same-sex attraction), but does not mention the animosity found at the beginning of same-sex attraction. For example, a seven-year-old boy notices the brutality of his father toward his mother and toward himself. He therefore makes a vow to separate himself from his father, a process known as *defensive detachment*. But the boy still yearns for another older male person, i.e., for a father. Defensive detachment from one's father is followed by same-sex attraction to members of his own sex, preferably older men. Moberly discovered this ambivalence in years of research at Cambridge University in England on the early relationships of children.[6]

6. **As a pastoral theologian, do you believe that the insights of Dr. Elizabeth Moberly are valuable in helping young persons with same-sex attraction (SSA) better understand themselves?**

Yes. Since the mid-1980s, I have counseled young persons with same-sex attraction, using Moberly's insights to help them realize that they *can* do something about their SSA. When a young person comes to understand that one does not deliberately choose to have this kind of attraction and that one can learn to reduce its power—and even, in

many cases, to get rid of it—he or she is usually desirous
to work with both a spiritual counselor and a therapist
to accomplish this. The young person is happy to hear
that, according to Moberly's understanding, attraction to
persons of the same sex is not pathological. In fact, it is the
drive to restore the disrupted attachment to "a (parental)
love-source of the same sex" and thus "is not a problem,
but rather the attempted solution to the problem."[7] What
is pathological is the early hostile detachment from a
parental figure of the same sex, but one can repair, as it
were, the deprivations of the past through the cultivation
of celibate same-sex friendships.[8]

In helping persons with SSA to be chaste (which is the
principal goal of Courage), I have found Moberly's view
most helpful.[9] Seeking chastity is the necessary first step
away from SSA. The individual may not be able to recover
completely his natural heterosexual tendencies, but he or
she is moving in the correct spiritual direction. With God's
grace, he or she will be able not only to avoid same-sex
sins but also to develop interior chastity. (We will discuss
chastity at greater length in chapter 2.) Until such persons
have moved through the immature stage of their feelings
to a rightly ordered affectivity, the virtue they can develop
would more properly be called *continence*. One who has the
virtue of chastity must, by definition, have feelings that
are habitually moved in concert with reason. As long as a
person still has defensive detachment or a predominant
sexual attraction to persons of the same sex, there still
exists a major defect in the relation of feelings to reason.

7. **Having considered the definition of homosexuality, how can we understand the phenomenon of bisexuality?**

The term *bisexuality* is used to describe the behavior of persons who indulge in sexual activity with persons of both sexes. This clinical definition tells us little about the interior feelings of the individuals indulging in such behavior. As there are many diverse explanations of bisexuality in psychological literature, I will not try to explain this behavior on a theoretical level.

Pastoral experience has shown that we need to make a distinction between the emotional life of the person and his or her behavior. Generally speaking, the so-called bisexual person is capable of sexual-genital relations with either sex but is emotionally involved primarily with his or her own sex. With the proper counseling, in many cases, such persons can learn to control their same-sex desires and have a truly good relationship with their spouses and children.[10]

8. **Are there specific texts from Holy Scripture that refer to same-sex (i.e., homosexual) acts?**

Yes—and in all such texts, homosexual acts are condemned. The *Letter to the Bishops of the Catholic Church on the Pastoral Care of Homosexual Persons*, issued by the Congregation for the Doctrine of the Faith, cites the following passages: Genesis 19:4-11 (concerning the destruction of Sodom and Gomorrah for homosexual behavior), Leviticus 18:22, 20:13 (condemning sodomy as an abomination), and Romans 1:18-32 (condemning male and female homosexual acts).[11] In the new context of the confrontation between Christianity and the pagan society of his day, St. Paul uses homosexual behavior as an example of the blindness which has overcome mankind: see 1 Corinthians 6:9-10 (in which Paul teaches that those who commit homosexual acts shall not enter the kingdom of God) and 1 Timothy 1:9-10 (in which he repeats the warning given in 1 Corinthians). In Romans 1:26, female same-sex acts are also specifically condemned.

9. Is there another way, apart from the Bible, of demonstrating the immorality of homosexual acts?

In my pastoral approach to persons with same-sex attraction, I use what I consider a better argument. In Genesis, chapters 1 and 2, it is clear that God designed the human body in two forms, male and female, for the purposes of marriage and procreation. I consider what the Church teaches concerning the nature of the marital act and then ask whether homosexual acts can fulfill the purposes of marriage.

10. Do recent official Church documents teach the immorality of homosexual acts?

The *Catechism of the Catholic Church* states the Church's definitive position on homosexual activity:

> Basing itself on Sacred Scripture, which presents homosexual acts as acts of grave depravity, tradition has always declared that 'homosexual acts are intrinsically disordered.' They are contrary to the natural law. They close the sexual act to the gift of life. They do not proceed from a genuine affective and sexual complementarity. Under no circumstances can they be approved.[12]

As I note in my book *The Truth about Homosexuality*, the teachings of *Gaudium et Spes*, *Humanae Vitae*, and the *Catechism*, among others, show "that there are two inseparable purposes in the marital act: the permanent union of man and woman and the procreation of children."[13]

The moral argument against homosexual activity, then, "flows directly from the revealed teaching on marriage, namely, that the two purposes of human sexual activity are the permanent union of husband and wife and the procreation of children—two purposes inseparably connected. Since homosexual activity cannot achieve either of these purposes, it must be immoral by its very nature."[14] This leads us to conclude that "there is no comparison between heterosexual marriages and sex outside of marriage, including same-sex unions."[15]

11. What texts of the Bible shed light on the nature of marriage?

The first two chapters of Genesis contain the foundational texts on marriage. Genesis 1:27-28, the first account of creation, states, "So God created man in his own image, in the image of God he created him; male and female he created them. And God blessed them, and God said to them, 'Be fruitful and multiply, and fill the earth and subdue it.'" In the second creation account, Genesis 2:23-24, God presents Eve to Adam, and Adam exclaims, "'This at last is bone of my bones and flesh of my flesh; she shall be called Woman, because she was taken out of Man.' Therefore a man leaves his father and his mother and cleaves to his wife, and they become one flesh." Notice how these two texts describe the communion of two bodies and the procreation of a child (see Genesis 4:1, the birth of Cain).

In the New Testament, Jesus reaffirms the norm proclaimed in Genesis. The gospel of Matthew 19:3-7 records that the Pharisees asked Jesus whether a man may divorce his wife on any pretext whatsoever. Jesus responds: "Have you not read that he who made them from the beginning made them male and female, and said, 'For this reason a man shall leave his father and mother and be joined to his wife, and the two shall become one'? So they are no longer two but one. What therefore God has joined together, let no man put asunder."

Ephesians, chapter 5, is a sublime passage in which the husband is compared with Christ and the wife with the Church. When St. Paul wishes to express the love that Christ has for the Church, he turns to the heterosexual love of husband and wife: "Husbands, love your wives, as Christ loved the church and gave himself up for her, that he might sanctify her...Even so husbands should love their wives as their own bodies" (Eph 5:25, 5:28). Then, St. Paul quotes Genesis 2:24: "For this reason a man shall leave his father and mother and be joined to his wife" (Eph 5:31). Thus, the Genesis norm of permanent heterosexual union is reaffirmed.

12. Could you recommend a book that gives a comprehensive treatment of the Bible's teachings concerning homosexual behavior?

The best book on the subject of the Bible and homosexual behavior is Dr. Robert A. J. Gagnon's *The Bible and Homosexual Practice* (Nashville: Abingdon Press, 2001). It treats the Scriptural texts on the subject thoroughly, and it supports the teachings of the Church in explaining passages of both the Old and New Testaments. This is a book that belongs in every library with books on homosexuality.[16]

13. Not all people believe in divine revelation. What approach does one take in speaking to non-believers about the morality of homosexual acts?

In speaking to people who do not believe in divine revelation, it is necessary to use arguments from the *natural moral law*.

The natural moral law is a law within the human person which begins to work when a child reaches the age of reason. It is the voice of conscience, helping us to distinguish right from wrong. It is right reason in operation. St. Paul refers to the natural moral law in Romans 2:14-15 when he says that the Gentiles who do not know the law of Moses have this law written in their hearts.

14. What are some natural moral law arguments against homosexual acts?

In accord with the natural moral law, the majority of men and women have a natural physical attraction to the opposite sex, and this attraction is meant to lead to an intimate permanent union of a man and a woman in marriage who look forward to children. We call this *complementarity*. With this is mind, let us consider the arguments of philosopher Michael Pakaluk. He argues against homosexual acts from the meaning of marital intercourse, "which has a special status that makes it different from other human activities. ...We say sex is special because it is a sign of the union of the *persons* who engage in sex. The sign is the union of bodies, and the sign signifies the union of persons. Thus, it is correct to say that when a man and woman engage in sex, the union of their bodies signifies the union of their selves."[17] Pakaluk adds that "sexual intercourse has a certain meaning independent of our choices; it signifies a union of selves."[18] Thus, we cannot change the objective meaning of sexual intercourse.

"Since, moreover, sexual intercourse between a man and a woman has a reproductive character, the act tends to produce offspring who combine the characteristics of husband and wife, and in so doing promote the unity of the spouses. As we know, homosexual intercourse has no such power."[19]

Other arguments can be developed. There cannot be a true communion of bodies in homosexual-genital intercourse. Some years ago a mother who was part of a team conducting an engagement encounter retreat privately asked me about homosexual behavior: "How do they do it?" I described how they did it, and she just smiled at me as she said, "The parts don't fit."

NOTES

1   Gerard van den Aardweg, *On the Origins and Treatment of Homosexuality* (New York: Praeger, 1986), p. 1.

2   Elizabeth R. Moberly, *Homosexuality: A New Christian Ethic* (Cambridge, England: James Clarke, 1983), p. 2.

3   John F. Harvey, O.S.F.S., *The Homosexual Person* (San Francisco: Ignatius Press, 1987), p. 28.

4   Moberly, *Homosexuality: A New Christian Ethic*, quoted in Harvey, *The Homosexual Person*, p. 28.

5   Harvey, *The Homosexual Person*, p. 28.

6   Ibid., pp. 28, 29.

7   Elizabeth Moberly, *Psychogenesis: The Early Development of Gender Identity* (London: Routledge and Kegan Paul, 1983), p. x.

8   Moberly, *Homosexuality*, pp. 28, 29.

9   For a more detailed account of Moberly's theory, consult chapter three of *The Homosexual Person*, pp. 38-48.

10 John F. Harvey, O.S.F.S., *The Truth about Homosexuality* (San Francisco: Ignatius Press, 1996), pp. 158-159.

11 Congregation for the Doctrine of the Faith, *Letter to the Bishops of the Catholic Church on the Pastoral Care of Homosexual Persons* (1986), nos. 6-8; see also *Persona Humana*, no. 8.

12 *Catechism of the Catholic Church (CCC)*, trans. United States Catholic Conference (1994), no. 2357.

13 Harvey, *The Truth About Homosexuality*, p. 124.

14 Ibid., p. 304.

15 Ibid., p. 127.

16 Available at http://www.amazon.com.

17 Harvey, *The Truth About Homosexuality*, p. 133.

18   Ibid.

19   Ibid.

CHAPTER 2

Helping Those with Same-Sex Attraction Live a Chaste Life: Pastoral Considerations

1. **Just so we're clear: Could you again describe the condition of homosexuality?**

Homosexuality is a persistent genital attraction to persons of the same sex. Persistent indicates that the physical attraction carries over into adulthood.[1] It is well known that many teenagers who think they are homosexual become physically attracted to persons of the other sex as they enter adulthood. It may happen that a person has a predominant attraction to persons of his own sex and a weaker attraction to persons of the other sex, or that he has a predominant attraction to persons of the other sex and a weaker attraction to persons of his own sex. The vast majority of men and women, however, about ninety-eight percent, have a strong physical attraction to members of the other sex and no significant physical attraction to their own.[2]

When an adult person perceives that his persistent, predominant attractions are toward members of his own sex, he may regard himself as having same-sex attraction. This does not mean that he will always have such attraction. Contemporary research indicates that some individuals do regain their heterosexual inclinations (about one out of three adults), but the majority remain with homosexual inclinations. We shall examine this later.

Genesis 1:27-28 and 2:18-24 speak of God creating man and woman, ordering them to increase and multiply and to form a union of two in one flesh. In other words, God placed in man and woman this natural attraction to draw them together, so that they would be willing to make a permanent commitment to one another in a two-in-one-flesh union, which would lead to children and family.

By way of contrast, same-sex couples are not able to have a true physical union, and their attempts to do so are not capable of bringing a child into existence. Such acts distort the meaning of human sexuality; they are violations of the virtue of chastity which is so necessary for union with Jesus Christ.

In this regard, distinguished Oxford University scholar John Finnis sums up the arguments from the natural moral law: "The commitment of a man and a woman to each other in the sexual union of marriage is intrinsically good and reasonable, and is incompatible with sex relationships outside of marriage."[3]

2.   **I notice you use "same-sex attraction" rather the popular terms "gay" or "lesbian." Is this intentional?**

Yes. I avoid using the terms "gay" and "lesbian" for good reason. An individual is more than a sexual inclination. An individual is a *person*, a creature made in the image and likeness of God, with intelligence and free will, destined for eternal life, and when baptized, a brother or sister of Christ. To refer to him or her as a "homosexual" is to reduce that person to a sexual tendency. A human being is far more than that in the mystery of his or her personhood.

The terms "gay" and "lesbian" are an even further reduction of a person's own wondrous complexity. Those who refer to themselves as "gay" or "lesbian" regard their sexual attraction as the most important mark of their identity. Whether one is born this way or not does not matter to such individuals. They claim, "This is the way I am and always will be. I must associate with people like myself and eventually find an ideal partner with whom I can settle down in a 'monogamous relationship.' I will work to bring about a society where same-sex unions are given the same privileges as heterosexual marriages."

All three forms of self-identification—homosexual, gay, and lesbian—fail to describe who one *really* is as a person. Far from being a merely academic question, how you regard yourself as a person has much to do with how you see yourself and how you set your personal goals for the future. Your self-image greatly influences your behavior.

3. **But doesn't the phrase "same-sex attraction" mean the same thing?**

No. Describing such persons as having "same-sex attraction" (as opposed to being "gay" or "lesbian") places the emphasis on the uniqueness of the person rather than on a sub-rational tendency which may change as the person matures. In contemporary discourse, people speak of their homosexual "orientation." Unfortunately, among many people with same-sex attraction, this term has the connotation of immutability, unchangeableness. But that is not the case with many individuals, particularly with teenagers who may seem so sure of themselves in declaring their homosexuality or lesbianism, only to gravitate in a few years into a love relationship with a person of the opposite sex.

The difficulty with labeling oneself is that it restricts one's options and vision. The Congregation for the Doctrine of the Faith's letter *On the Pastoral Care of Homosexual Persons (PCHP)* makes this point very well: "Today the Church provides a badly needed context for the care of the human person when she refuses to consider the person as 'heterosexual' or 'homosexual,' and insists that every person has a fundamental identity: creature of God, and by His grace, His child and heir to eternal life."[4]

Thus, the condition of homosexuality does not take away from one's God-given dignity as a creature of God, nor does it change the fact that a baptized person is a brother or sister of Christ, with the hope of eternal life. On the human level, moreover, to adopt the perspective of Dr. Joseph Nicolosi, author of *Healing Homosexuality*, one should regard himself as a heterosexual with a homosexual problem.[5]

God does not make people homosexual; God permits this particular suffering to come to people for His own mysterious reasons. One should avoid the temptation to hate oneself, to indulge in self-pity, and to be angry with God because one has been mistakenly led to believe that God made him homosexual. Regarding oneself as worthless because of same-sex attraction is really a form of homophobia (i.e., an unreasonable fear and sometimes a hatred of persons with same-sex attraction) and even hatred of oneself.

Many Americans have unreasonable fears of persons known to be homosexual because the homosexual condition is confused with pedophilia, or is associated with AIDS, or is thought to be freely chosen by the person. The Church, however, exhorts us to provide the person with same-sex attraction with a special pastoral care, treating him with love and respect: "The intrinsic dignity of each person must always be respected in word, in action, and in law."[6]

4. **You have discussed those who refer to themselves as "gays" and "lesbians," but what about "bisexuals"?**

As we have seen previously, the term *bisexual* simply describes a form of behavior in which one is physically attracted, to varying degrees, to genital acts with both sexes. From his research, A.P. McDonald states that one will look in vain for a precise definition of bisexuality; he also raises questions about considering bisexuality as homosexuality.[7]

One must distinguish between the emotional life of the person and his behavior. From my pastoral experience, I usually regard such a person as a homosexual. Generally, the bisexual person is capable of sexual-genital relations with either sex but is emotionally involved principally with members of his own sex. If, on the other hand, he is emotionally attracted to a person of the other sex while merely seeking physical pleasure from a person of his own sex, often with fantasies of the other sex, he is heterosexual. Emotional attraction to a person of the same sex expressed in physical desire for union seems to be the main criterion of the homosexual inclination.

This is a pastoral problem. In some instances, if the person is married, seeking an annulment (i.e., an official declaration that what what was thought to be a valid marriage is not) may be the pastoral solution. In other instances, the person can learn to control his same-sex desires and to relate well to his spouse and children.

5.   What causes same-sex attraction?

Since I have discussed this question in my first book, *The Homosexual Person*,[8] which reviews the brilliant work of Elizabeth Moberly and the insights of Gerard van den Aardweg, I will reference here several other books which will be insightful concerning the origins and treatment of same-sex attraction.[9] Suffice it to say that there are many theories concerning the beginnings of such attraction. Later, I will discuss references concerning the possibility of recovering one's natural heterosexual inclinations.

A difficulty for persons with same-sex attraction is that there are often traumas in their family background which they experienced as children and adolescents and which remain deep in their emotional life, rendering the practice of chastity more arduous.

In counseling adolescent men and women with same-sex attraction, I have come to understand why chastity is such a challenge for them. Why isn't a particular boy attracted to girls, as are his peers? Why isn't a particular girl attracted to boys? Feelings of shame arise as such adolescents struggle with same-sex lust. But there is no one with whom they can discuss their secret. As a consequence, they often flee into the world of sexual fantasy, where they find temporary relief in the practice of masturbation. Today, through the Internet, they can find websites that cater to their fantasy life.

Heterosexual youth have little difficulty discussing sexual temptations with their peers or with older counselors. They realize that they suffer the same sort of sexual temptations as their companions. They can seek spiritual direction; with prayer they can practice the virtue of chastity.

Despite all these difficulties, however, persons with same-sex attraction do learn to live chastely—but not without a struggle. They practice continence, which St. Thomas calls an imperfect virtue in comparison with chastity. But it is still a virtue. I call it "white-knuckled chastity," because of the fierce battle taking place in the person's soul. The task of Courage leaders is to help members to move from continence to interior chastity, or chastity of the heart.

St. Augustine sums up the teaching of the Church on chastity by saying, "God does not command impossible things, but in commanding, He admonishes us both to do what you can do, and to seek His grace to do what you cannot do."[10]

This truth—that God always gives the individual the graces to do whatever He commands—is the solemn teaching of the sixth session of the Council of Trent. Today, some within the Church attempt to make the person with same-sex attraction an exception to the law of chastity binding all human beings. This is why Courage came into existence at the invitation of the late Terence Cardinal Cooke, and why its primary goal is to teach interior chastity, or chastity of the heart.

6.   Can a distinction be made between a homosexual inclination and homosexual acts?

Yes, though many individuals with same-sex attraction insist that the inclination to homosexual acts and the behavior cannot be separated. These individuals often believe that they were born with this inclination and that it is natural to them and therefore ought to be expressed with someone of their own sex in homosexual acts. (Note that the inclination to homosexual acts is not sinful in itself, unless one freely consents to these desires.) Having become *addicted* to homosexual acts, they believe that they cannot control their sexual desires. Even if some have come to admit that there is a distinction between inclinations and acts, many still believe that they are incapable of controlling such desires. One notices a similar despair in the situation of alcoholics and those addicted to pornography.[11]

Throughout many years of pastoral practice, I have never met anyone who *chose* to have a homosexual inclination. For this reason, the Church calls this inclination an "objective disorder." The inclination is "objective" in the sense that it develops in the psychological makeup of the individual, and it is a "disorder" because if one yields to these desires, one commits an act which is a serious violation of the law of God because homosexual acts are not, and can never be, in accord with the intent of the Creator of human sexuality. To sum up, the inclination to same-sex desires is not a sin, but it makes the practice of chastity more difficult.

In other instances, such individuals may have been brainwashed by gay propaganda. In all these situations there is the nagging fear that one is not able to be chaste.

St. Augustine describes in his *Confessions* a similar fear of not being able to overcome the habit of lust.[12]

7. **So are people with same-sex attraction responsible for their behavior?**

We must always distinguish objective morality from the responsibility of the person giving consent to such desires and acts. Previously, we have seen the arguments from both the Old and New Testaments which demonstrate that the objective criterion for the exercise of sexuality is the state of marriage. This led to the conclusion that all other genital acts, including homosexual acts, are immoral. The point was further developed that the natural moral law supports the thesis of Holy Scripture that acts of intercourse may take place only in the state of marriage. From both Holy Scripture and natural moral law we draw the conclusion that homosexual acts are always, by their very nature, seriously immoral.

When we turn, however, to the person who has same-sex attraction, we are considering his personal responsibility for his acts. How much freedom does a person with same-sex tendencies have to avoid consent to homosexual lust? In most cases, he has sufficient freedom, buttressed by grace, to avoid consent to such lustful desires and acts. Where there is sufficient freedom, there is likewise responsibility.

In this regard, heterosexual persons should be very careful not to make harsh judgments about persons with same-sex attraction. From many years of working with such persons, I have come to see that many environmental factors contribute to their lapse into a homosexual way of living. Through the help of God, many persons who began their adult lives in homosexual activity have now come to learn how to live chastely. Moral theologians, in their analysis of this question, are aware of the many factors which reduce human freedom and consequently may lessen the culpability of such persons.

8.   Can it be said that same-sex attraction is an addiction?

In itself, same-sex attraction is not an addiction, but it can and often does become one. An *addiction* is a state of mind in which the person is not able to control his actions despite the fact that he has repeatedly tried to do so. He may be aware of the immorality of his actions and yet not be able to do anything about it.

There are two working definitions of addiction which I have found pastorally beneficial. I shall apply these definitions to two kinds of addiction which are serious problems, not only for some Courage members, but for many others who suffer the effects of original sin. John Bradshaw, a reliable psychologist, understands compulsion or addiction as "a pathological relationship to any mood altering experience that has life damaging consequences." One observes that the individual has lost control of a certain behavior and that he has consciously tried to rid himself of it, with little or no success.

Step one of Alcoholics Anonymous, for example, refers to addiction when it says, "I am an alcoholic, and I am powerless over this condition." The classic example of a pathological relationship (addiction) is the alcoholic, but one finds the same difficulty in persons who are addicted to pornography, masturbation, or homosexual behavior.

The second descriptive definition sheds further light on the meaning of addiction: "A state of compulsion, obsession, or preoccupation that enslaves a person's will or desire. Addiction sidetracks and eclipses the energy of our deepest and truest desire for love and goodness. We succumb because the energy of our desire becomes attached, nailed to specific behaviors, objects, or people. Attachment...is the process that enslaves desire and creates the state of addiction."[13]

The first definition deals with the observable fact that the addict has lost control of his life in a significant area, while the second definition searches the interior sources in the addict for his behavior.

An addict has the responsibility to seek proper help to regain the freedom of his will through prayer and spiritual support groups. Both Sexaholics Anonymous (SA) and Courage can help him regain self-respect, a strengthening of the will by the power of grace, and, in the course of prayer, what I call chastity of the heart, i.e., learning to be chaste out of love for Christ.

9.   **Should persons with same-sex attraction seek professional therapy?**

One can encourage such persons to use professional therapy as a means of drawing further and further away from same-sex attraction, and thus from temptations to sin, but I hesitate to make this an obligation for everyone. Besides professional therapy, there are other ways of reducing the strength of same-sex attraction, such as prayer, group meetings, strong friendships with both heterosexual and same-sex-attracted persons, and the pursuit of ideals, as I have found in persons whom

I counseled over the years. Again, many people cannot afford professional therapy over a long period of time; nevertheless, Courage has referred many of its members to clinical psychologists and psychiatrists from the very beginning of its existence.

10. Can individuals truly be "cured" from same-sex attraction or must they live with it for the rest of their lives?

In the December 2003 issue of the *NARTH Bulletin* (published by the National Association for Research and Therapy of Homosexuality), Roy Waller and Linda Nicolosi sum up the results of a study conducted by Dr. Robert L. Spitzer.[14] A summary of his research will be helpful to those interested in this important issue.[15]

Spitzer challenges the notion that homosexual orientation cannot be changed. In his study—which included 200 respondents of both genders (143 males and fifty-seven females)—he reported changes from homosexual to heterosexual orientation lasting five years or more. It was a sixteen-month study of structured telephone interviews. "Although examples of complete change of orientation were not common, the majority of the participants did report change from a predominantly, or exclusively, homosexual orientation before therapy to a predominantly or exclusively heterosexual orientation in the previous year as a result of reparative therapy."[16]

Spitzer's findings run contrary to the position of the major health organizations in the United States, which claim that "there is no scientific basis for believing psychotherapy effective in addressing same-sex attraction. Yet Spitzer reports evidence of change in both sexes, although female participants reported significantly more change than did male participants."[17]

It is interesting that the average age of the participants was forty-two for males, forty-four for females, and that seventy-six percent of the males and forty-seven percent of females were married. Ninety-seven percent came from a Christian background, and ninety-three percent believed that religion was either "extremely" or very important in their lives. Forty-one percent had been "openly gay" at some point before beginning therapy, and more than a third of both males and females reported that they had seriously considered suicide at some time in their lives because of dissatisfaction with their "unwanted attractions."[18]

Spitzer asked the participants about their motivation for wanting to change. The majority indicated that they did not find the homosexual lifestyle to be emotionally satisfying. Seventy-nine percent of both genders held that homosexual activity conflicted with their religious beliefs, and sixty-seven percent of men and thirty-five percent of women regarded homosexual behavior to be in conflict with their desire to remain married.[19]

Most of the respondents stated that they still occasionally struggle with unwanted same-sex attraction. Only eleven percent of the men and thirty-seven percent of the women said that they were completely cured. Nevertheless, they were able to develop an affective attachment to a person of the other sex.

Spitzer responds to a frequently repeated objection of the "gay" media, namely, that the therapist harms the person with same-sex attraction if he uses reparative therapy. He sees no evidence of harm; on the contrary, his clients expressed their appreciation for the therapy, which helped them in a variety of ways beyond changing sexual orientation. He has appealed to the American Psychiatric Association, requesting that it stop applying a double standard in its "discouragement of reorientation therapy while it actively encourages gay affirmative therapy to confirm and solidify a gay identity."[20]

Spitzer also rejects the notion that persons seek reorientation therapy because they are driven by guilt. He stresses that "the ability to make such a choice should be considered fundamental to client autonomy and self-determination."

It is my hope that others will seek to replicate and build on Spitzer's research. One may follow up research in this field by visiting the NARTH website.[21] While Courage leaders continue to give spiritual direction to Courage groups in our country, it also cooperates with therapists associated with NARTH in helping members of Courage to move further away from same-sex attraction, and, if possible, to recover their natural heterosexual inclinations.

NOTES

1. In this book I only speak of homosexual inclinations in adults. With reference to signs of homosexuality in children, the reader may wish to examine the following two interviews: "Recognizing and Treating Same-Sex Attractions in Children," Zenit News Agency, November 16, 2003, http://www.zenit.org/article-8708?l=english; and "Source of Same-Sex Attractions in Children: Parenting and Social Influences," Zenit News Agency, January 24, 2004, http://www.zenit.org/article-17451?l=english.

2. Harvey, *The Homosexual Person*, pp. 27-30.

3. John Finnis, "Law, Morality, and Sexual Orientation," *Notre Dame Law Review* 69 (1994): 1062.

4. Congregation for the Doctrine of the Faith, *On the Pastoral Care of Homosexual Persons (PCHP)* (1986), no. 16.

5. Joseph Nicolosi, Ph.D., *Healing Homosexuality* (Northvale, NJ: Jason Aronson, 1997)

6. *PCHP*, no. 10.

7. *Journal of Homosexualilty* 6 (1981): 21ff.

8. Harvey, *The Homosexual Person*.

9. Harvey, "Some Recent Theories Concerning the Origins of Homosexuality," *The Homosexual Person*, pp. 37-63. See Elizabeth Moberly, *Psychogenesis: The Very Early Development of Gender Identity* (Cambridge, England: Cambridge University Press, 1983); Gerard van den Aardweg, *On the Origins and Treatment of Homosexuality* (New York: Praeger, 1986); and *The Battle for Normality: A Guide for Self Therapy for Homosexuality* (San Francisco: Ignatius, 1997); Joseph Nicolosi, *Reparative Therapy of Male Homosexuality* (Northvale, NJ: Jason Aronson, 1991); Jeffrey Satinover, *Homosexuality and the Politics of Truth* (Grand Rapids, MI: Baker Books, 1996).

[10] St. Augustine, as quoted by Pope Pius XII in *Questions Concerning Married Life* (NCWC: 1951), ch. 2, p. 16, par. 40. The quotation also applies to the person with same-sex attractions seeking to be chaste.

[11] See the section on pornography in chapter 3.

[12] See John F. Harvey, O.S.F.S., *Moral Theology of the Confessions of St. Augustine* (Washington, DC: Catholic University of America Press, 1951), pp. 83-85, 107-108.

[13] Gerald R May, M.D., *Addiction and Grace* (New York: Harper and Row, 1988), p.14.

[14] Linda Nicolosi and Ray Waller, "Spitzer Study Just Published: Evidence Found of Effectiveness of Reorientation Therapy," *NARTH Bulletin* 12, no. 3 (December 2003): 1-2. Interestingly, in 1973, Spitzer took the lead in proposing that homosexuality no longer be classified as a mental illness but rather as another form of normality. That year, he helped persuade the American Psychiatric Association to remove the term "homosexuality" from its *Diagnostic and Statistical Manual (DSM)*, the official list of mental disorders. In 2003, though, he reversed his position; see *Archives of Sexual Behavior* 32, no. 5 (October 2003): 203-417.

[15] The following paragraphs summarize the article, referred to above, by Nicolosi and Waller.

[16] Ibid.

[17] Ibid.

[18] Ibid.

[19] Ibid., n. 11.

[20] Ibid.

[21] NARTH website, http://www.narth.com. Or write to them at 16633 Ventura Blvd., Suite 1340, Encino, CA 91436 or call (818) 789-4440.

CHAPTER 3

The Pastoral Challenges of
Masturbation and Pornography

1. **Why discuss masturbation and pornography in a book on same-sex attraction?**

Many people with same-sex attraction struggle with these issues. In addition, I believe that persons with same-sex attraction have more difficulty with masturbation than do heterosexual persons. Why is this? The person with same-sex attraction often does not want to admit even to himself that he has this homosexual inclination, sometimes withdrawing into an intense fantasy life with compulsive masturbation. He fears admitting this inclination to others and considers masturbation a safe alternative. Since, moreover, such a person has more difficulty finding intimacy and friendship than do heterosexuals, it is not surprising that he tends to form such habits.

In my pastoral work, I have observed the close connection between the habits of pornography and masturbation. Certainly, in more recent years, due to the availability of pornography on the Internet, addiction to these two habits has become more widespread than ever before. Many have been led to moral despair in the sense that they no longer try to control these habits. To be sure, the heart of the problem is complex, and the Internet is only an accessory. We will first examine the problem of masturbation.

2.   How would you describe the pastoral problem of masturbation? What harm does it do?

Masturbation has also been called *self-abuse, onanism,* and, in the euphemisms of secular textbooks, *self-pleasuring.* Father Benedict Groeschel, C.F.R., uses the term *autoeroticism* for the activity of older adolescents and adults "who for a variety of reasons are driven in on oneself and find a substitute from real living in this symbolic and intensely frustrating behavior." He reserves the term *masturbation* to denote actions that take place in sleep (or semi-sleep), as well as the actions of child and early adolescent sexual behavior. In making this distinction, Father Benedict indicates that there is more awareness and free will in autoerotic behavior.[1]

In his classic article on the Church's moral teaching about masturbation in the *New Catholic Encyclopedia,* Father Joseph Farraher, S.J., describes it as the "stimulation of the external sex organs to a point of climax or orgasm by oneself, by movements of the hand or other physical contacts or by sexually-stimulating pictures or imaginations . . . or by a combination of physical and psychical stimulation."[2] In a broader sense, this includes mutual masturbation, in which persons touch one another's genitalia.

Perhaps one of the most insightful views on masturbation is found in a letter of C. S. Lewis:

> For me the real evil of masturbation would be that it takes an appetite, which, in lawful use, leads an individual out of himself to complete (and correct) his own personality in that of another (and finally in children and even in grandchildren) and turns it back, sends it back into the prison of one's self, there to keep a harem of imaginary brides. And this harem,

once admitted, works against his ever getting out and really uniting with a real woman. For the harem is always accessible, always subservient, calls for no sacrifices or adjustments and can be endowed with erotic and psychological attractions which no real woman can rival.[3]

This quotation can be applied to women as well as men, expressing the meaning of masturbation as a personal flight from reality into the prison of lust.

3.   **In recent decades, haven't some experts—including some theologians and psychologists—questioned the Church's traditional teaching on masturbation?**

Yes. The opponents of Church teaching on masturbatory activity, however, fail to draw the distinction between objective gravity and subjective guilt. As we shall show, the act of masturbation is a serious violation of natural moral law. Such a violation is serious matter, but it becomes a mortal sin only when the person is fully aware of the gravity of the act and has freely consented to it. The authentic teaching of the Church is stated in the 1975 document *Persona Humana* of the Congregation for the Doctrine of the Faith:

> The teaching of the Church is frequently doubted, if not expressly denied...This opinion, however, is contrary to both the teaching and the pastoral practice of the Church. Whatever force there may be in certain biological and philosophical arguments put forward from time to time by theologians, the fact remains that both the Magisterium of the Church, in the course of a constant tradition, and the moral sense of the faithful have been in no doubt, and have firmly maintained that masturbation is an intrinsically and gravely disordered action.[4]

Many psychologists and some moral theologians have objected to this teaching, believing that the widespread practice of masturbation, particularly among males, makes it difficult for moralists to continue to hold to the traditional position. It seems to them to be in conflict with common sense. Such moralists downplay the issue of the objective gravity of the act, taking refuge in the fact that, on the pastoral level, many people lack full awareness and full freedom and this prevents such acts from being mortally sinful.

Father Farraher argues cogently from constant Church teaching that masturbation is a serious violation of the moral order if one is fully aware of the malice of the act and does it. Since it does not fulfill the purposes of union and procreation to which the marital act is ordained, it is a seriously disordered and sinful act.

In his *New Catholic Encyclopedia* article, Farraher is very exact about what constitutes grave malice when he writes, "For a person to be formally guilty of a mortal sin of masturbation, his act must be a fully deliberate choice of what he fully realizes is seriously sinful. If such an act is done with only partial realization, or partial consent of the will, it is a venial sin," and "if there is no free choice of the will there is no guilt of sin at all, even if the person is aware of what he is doing."[5] The latter statement would apply to a compulsive act of any kind.

Farraher corrects the misunderstanding that many Catholics have that if they experience sexual stimulation, however unwillingly, they have committed mortal sin. Among today's generation, however, I do not believe that many suffer from such guilt; if anything, many are surprised to learn that masturbation is sinful. It is necessary, then, to instruct the faithful with Father Farraher's careful distinctions so as to avoid anxiety of conscience on the one hand, and a mindless laxism on the other.

4. **But the Bible doesn't say anything about masturbation, does it?**

In Sacred Scripture, one does not find texts which explicitly refer to masturbation, but, as William E. May points out, "the condemnation of [this] sin can be deduced indirectly from the teaching of St. Paul" where he condemns wicked passion in general and in which moral theologians find a reference to the solitary sin.[6] Thus, Paul advises marriage: "But if [the unmarried] cannot exercise self-control, they should marry. For it is better to marry than to be aflame with passion" (1 Cor 7:9). The following Pauline texts also may be understood as *implicit* condemnation of masturbation: 2 Corinthians 7:1; Galatians 5:23; and 1 Thessalonians 4:4. It is important to note, according to Dr. May, that although Scripture does not condemn this sin by name, "the tradition of the Church has rightly understood it to be condemned in the New Testament when the latter speaks of 'impurity,' 'unchasteness' and other vices contrary to chastity and continence."[7]

5. **Given that masturbation is fairly common—especially among adolescents—how can it be seriously wrong?**

Magisterial teaching responds to the objection that masturbation is not a grave moral disorder in certain circumstances. Adolescent masturbation is given as one of the examples. The Church has always acknowledged that circumstances alter cases and that there are degrees of responsibility in the different kinds of masturbation.

But, as the *Catechism of the Catholic Church* clearly teaches, the Church still holds that the act of masturbation remains objectively, seriously wrong (see *CCC* 2352). The Church distinguishes between the objective gravity of the act of masturbation and the personal responsibility of the agent. This important distinction enables us to hold to the traditional position, while making allowances for a variety of mitigating factors which can diminish the personal guilt of the masturbator, provided he is willing to do whatever may be necessary to overcome the bad habit, or in some cases, the compulsion.

In my years of pastoral experience I have yet to meet a penitent who did not want to rid himself of the habit of masturbation or who continues to deliberately masturbate. In practice, authors who hold that masturbation is not a grave matter are overawed by statistical studies, which show that the majority of teenage boys and a high percentage of teenage girls masturbate. These studies do not describe the frequency of masturbation or the state of conscience of the masturbator. They fail to take into account the contemporary phenomena of spiritual support groups to overcome sexual addictions, such as Sexaholics Anonymous (SA) and Sex and Love Addicts Anonymous. Both groups treat compulsive masturbation as a sexual addiction to be overcome through the practice of the Twelve Steps, adapted to sexual problems.

6. **Is there a difference between habit and compulsion in masturbation?**

Yes. On the pastoral level one must make a distinction between those who masturbate due to habit and those that do so from a true compulsion. By definition, the habitual masturbator still has some control over his actions, refraining from masturbating for long periods of time, relapsing for a short period. He may use masturbation as a substitute for sexual intercourse (or, in the case of those with same-sex attraction, for an act of sodomy). He is able, however, to stop the habit whenever he is motivated to do so, usually for religious reasons.

Loneliness and depression are powerful factors in both men and women with regard to this habit. In some cases, however, individuals cross the line from habit into compulsion; that is to say, they find themselves masturbating very frequently despite the use of ordinary means to avoid it. Actually, as the compulsive masturbator practices the Twelve Steps, he recognizes the latent insincerity and desire for sexual satisfaction in his previous protestations that he really did not want to do it. Part of healing is becoming more honest with regard to one's motivations. The following poem says it all:

"Autobiography in Five Short Chapters"
by Portia Nelson

1. I walk down the street.
There is a deep hole in the sidewalk.
I fall in.
I'm lost...I am helpless.
It isn't my fault.
It takes forever to find a way out.

2. I walk down the same street.
There is a deep hole in the sidewalk.
I pretend I don't see it.
I fall in again.
I can't believe I am in the same place.

But it isn't my fault.
It still takes a long time to get out.

3. I walk down the same street.
There is a deep hole in the sidewalk.
I still fall in...It's a habit.
My eyes are open.
I know where I am.
It is my fault.
I get out immediately.

4. I walk down the same street.
There is a deep hole in the sidewalk.
I walk around it.

5. I walk down another street.

Masturbation is a complex phenomenon. As the Congregation for Catholic Education has pointed out, one of the causes of masturbation is sexual imbalance, and "efforts [in education] should be directed toward the causes rather than in attacking the problem directly."[8] This is a wise approach. We will not know why a person is burdened with this habit unless we know something about his background.

7.   **What leads a person to masturbate?**

From listening to people, one discerns that loneliness is a prime mover, leading the individual into isolation, fantasy, and masturbation. Loneliness is usually joined with feelings of deep self-hatred and anger. When the real world is harsh and forbidding, one turns to fantasy, and when one spends much time in a fantasy world, he becomes enslaved by sexual *objects* (for that is the way he sees other persons, as *objects*). Thereafter, he will flee to the unreal world of his imagination. This is the beginning of sexual addiction, so well described by Patrick Carnes in his book *Out of the Shadows.*[9]

So often the habit of masturbation becomes compulsive—that is to say, the person is unable to control the behavior in spite of great efforts to do so. Usually such a person needs therapy in conjunction with spiritual direction. Sometimes, however, the habit of masturbation is temporary and circumstantial. For example, as soon as an individual is out of a given environment, the tendency to masturbate disappears.

For example, a twenty-five-year-old nun was surrounded by older religious with whom there was no real communication, and in the summer-school environment she was living with religious of her own age. She gradually became aware that the temptation toward masturbation had disappeared when she was with religious her own age. She realized that the reason for the masturbation in the first place was that she was isolated and lonely in the first group, and now, engaged in real relationships in the summer-school environment, she felt no need to allow fantasy to take over. Other examples could be given in which masturbation is symptomatic of other underlying forces in the person's life. These symptoms—varied in terms of age, external circumstances of life, and interior dispositions—will be described and evaluated in a later section of this chapter.

Pastoral counselors and confessors are familiar with persons who masturbate daily in spite of their desire to be rid of the compulsion. Such individuals live with guilt and shame. They are not satisfied with the counselor's attempt to console them by saying they are not guilty of serous sin because they lack control over masturbation. They want to know what they can do to regain control over sexual impulses.

8.   **What can counselors do to help a person who suffers from compulsive masturbation?**

The first thing the counselor can do is to study sexual addiction and learn what can be done to help the compulsive masturbator. A writer on the subject, John Bradshaw, says that sexual addiction is a pseudo-relationship to a mind-altering sexual experience with destructive effects upon the self, and in some instances upon others as well.[10] Patrick Carnes explains it this way: "The addict substitutes a sick relationship to an event or process for a healthy relationship with others. The addict's relationship with a mood-altering [substance]...becomes central to his life."[11]

Carnes stresses the truth that people tend to confuse sexual addiction with pleasurable or frequent sexual activity. The difference is that ordinary people can learn to moderate their sexual behavior, while the addict cannot do so. He has lost the ability to say no, because his behavior is part of a cycle of thinking, feeling, and acting which he cannot control. Instead of enjoying sex as a self-affirming source of pleasure in marriage, the sex addict uses it as a relief from pain or from stress, similar to the way an alcoholic relies on alcohol. Contrary to love, the obsessional illness transforms sex into the primary need, for which all else may be sacrificed, including family, friends, health, safety, and work.

Despite all the obstacles to freedom found in addiction, there is hope for the compulsive masturbator for a couple of reasons:

1. He can come to understand that he is not a bad person, but rather someone suffering from an illness, which can be treated and overcome. As long as he hates himself and considers himself as worthless (shame), he believes that he is hopeless (despair).

2. With the help of a spiritual director and therapist he can realize that he can overcome his addiction. He will also need the practice of the Twelve Steps through participation in group support meetings. In this respect, he can find invaluable help at meetings of Sexaholics Anonymous and Courage.

In asserting that there is hope for the compulsive masturbator, I rely not upon mere book knowledge, but upon the experience of sending persons to Sexaholics Anonymous, as well as working with members of Courage in New York. The primary purpose of Courage is to teach members how to be chaste. Courage works with some members who have been addicted to masturbation. Improvement in the practice of chastity does not take place overnight. It is a gradual process, sometimes with painful relapses, demanding regular consultations with a spiritual director, heartfelt admission of personal powerlessness, faithful attendance at meetings, utter honesty in talking about oneself, and the daily practice of meditation or prayer of the heart.

The addict must make a distinction between responsibility for his past actions and responsibility for his present and future actions. It is, however, practically impossible for him to make an accurate moral evaluation of his past actions. We have no way of categorizing the kinds and degrees of compulsive sexual behavior or, for that matter, of any other sort of compulsive behavior. Each compulsive masturbator comes from a different set of life circumstances with a different pattern of personality traits. As Rudolph Allers wrote years ago, and as other authors would hold, "We cannot know anything about the nature of the alleged irresistible impulses unless we know all we can find about the total personality."[12] As in other forms of addiction, compulsive masturbation begins in fantasy, and the fantasy fills the mind in such a way that other thoughts and counteracting motives have no real chance of distracting the person from the pleasurable images which lead to masturbation. Consciousness is narrowed to one idea, one image. This is compulsion in the full sense.[13]

9. **You use the phrase "compulsion in the full sense." Is there another type of compulsion?**

Yes. There is another form of compulsion in which one is immersed in the object of his desire, feeling that he must give in to the impulse to get some physical relief or he will suffer great pain. Here, the person is aware that he *can* resist and knows that there is another option. He or she possesses some freedom, but to an insufficient degree to constitute serious guilt. This is even truer when persons struggle against the impulse to masturbate when they are trying to sleep at night, or when they are surprised by temptation in the middle of the night or upon awakening in the morning.

As a confessor, one encounters priests and religious who are obsessed with sexual fantasies, feeling compelled to give in to them. Still others who find no pleasure in masturbation feel driven to do so. In all these situations, I recommend that the person: 1) seek out a therapist who agrees with Church teaching, and 2) go regularly to spiritual support systems where one can discuss these painful conflicts and compulsive tendencies.

10. But hasn't the person consented in some way or at some point, maybe at the very beginning?

This is "the moment of truth" theory, and can apply to either compulsive or non-compulsive masturbators. According to Allers, the so-called irresistible impulse becomes such even before it is *fully* developed. The person has the uneasy feeling something is going to happen, as he is involved in some form of fantasy, which often includes pornographic literature, images, or videos. He realizes that he ought to get rid of the fantasy or the pornography, but he does not. Perhaps on the unconscious level there is a drive to find satisfaction in masturbation, which the person will not admit on the conscious level. In this situation Allers holds that in some way the person is responsible for not taking advantage of the moment of truth and for allowing himself to be enslaved by desire. "This action may, therefore, not carry any responsibility, and nonetheless, not be excusable, because in fact the person *has assented to its development*."[14] As we have learned from Portia Nelson's "Autobiography in Five Short Chapters," healing involves becoming more honest with oneself.

11. You mention "becoming honest with oneself." So there are some dishonest ways to look at masturbation, aren't there?

Yes, there are. The most blatantly misleading approach is the attitude that teenagers will grow out of it. Many do not. Another myth is that if one practices masturbation, he is less likely to act out with another person of the other or same sex. Although this may be true in some instances, some have said that masturbation prepared them to act out sexually. In some situations, masturbation has been recommended as a way of relieving bodily tensions, like a form of sex therapy. It is not therapeutic, because the habit or the addiction of masturbatory behavior carries with it a heavy burden of guilt.

Mutual masturbation has been used by persons with same-sex attraction as "safe sex." Some may avoid AIDS in this way, but this is not "safe" in the spiritual order, because such actions are seriously sinful and may lead to "unsafe" sexual activity. Still other counselors minimize the problem, giving no advice except "not to worry about it." Indeed many priests, seminarians, and teachers of religion in Catholic schools regard even the habit of masturbation as a non-issue, or perhaps as a purely psychological problem. When will they wake up?

12. **What is the correct approach to deal with masturbation?**

The correct attitude is to treat masturbation, whether habitual or compulsive, as a problem open to a solution, provided the person follows a spiritual program. He must assume responsibility for his future. As he frees himself from the disorder by the grace of God, he also becomes more responsible. I have found the following directives to be useful:

   1. Help the person reflect upon the meaning of his life, hopes, accomplishments, disappointments, frustrations, and loneliness. Try to discover what is eating him. Masturbation is often symptomatic of restlessness in the soul, and this needs to be attacked first.

2. If he is drifting, provide him with a spiritual plan of life similar to the one I have written for persons with same-sex attraction. Actually, most of it is applicable to heterosexual persons with a sexual problem.

3. Make him aware that most human beings have a tendency to slip into pleasant worlds of fantasy when reality becomes harsh and bleak, and masturbation often flows out of such fantasy. The spiritual strategy is learning to bring oneself back from sexual fantasy into reality as soon as one notes that he is involved in sexual fantasy.

   One approach that works with some is to utter a short prayer, and then do something external and physical, such as work around the home, taking a walk, and so on. Have you ever found yourself in fantasies of anger, jealousy, or sex, and the telephone rings and, as you answer, the fantasy fades away? The art is to stay in reality.

4. Besides sharing the difficulty with a spiritual director, one should seek out a support group like Sexaholics Anonymous. Compulsive and habitual masturbators have found real friendship through these meetings. The cultivation of real friendships with real people significantly reduces the power of sexual fantasy, while giving one a sense of self-worth.

Two additional points should be made by priests and counselors in helping teenagers who think they may be homosexual or bisexual:

• First, one should examine the kind of fantasy which leads to masturbation in the young person. (Within the sacrament of penance, though, priests must exercise prudence and caution when questioning penitents regarding sins against the sixth commandment. Such questions would more more appropriately treated to spiritual direction.) Is the fantasy concerning children or teenagers? Does it have masochistic images, like being beaten by the other person or inflicting injury on the other? If so, the individual needs professional therapy.

• Second, if the individual considers himself bisexual because he has had sexual experiences with both sexes, one should help him to reflect upon his patterns of fantasy. If the fantasy is primarily of a heterosexual nature, chances are that the person is predominately heterosexual in orientation. If, on the other hand, fantasy is predominately homosexual in nature, it is likely at this point that he is fixated in a homosexual orientation. I qualify my position in this way because teenagers who fantasize about persons of the same sex may move out of this kind of fantasy in the course of their maturation, particularly with the help of therapy. It goes without saying that one should resist such fantasies.

13. Can masturbation lead to further problems?

The habit of masturbation renders many homosexual persons vulnerable to promiscuity: first, fantasy and masturbation; then cruising the haunts; and later, finding someone for a one-night stand. Thus, in group discussions persons with same-sex attraction, stress the seriousness of masturbation in their own lives, regarding a slip into this practice as a failure in their struggle for chastity.

With the AIDS epidemic, mutual masturbation has become the principal form of so-called "safe sex." Although it is considered "safe," it destroys the relationship of the person with God, and it also prevents the person from becoming sexually integrated with himself. Even when the habit of masturbation is involuntary, it still signifies a lack of integration within the person. Whether voluntary or involuntary, masturbation engenders deep feelings of guilt and shame in the person. It is necessary, then, to explore these feelings.

One needs to distinguish two different kinds of guilt: healthy and neurotic. When I have freely done something wrong, I should feel guilty for breaking the law of God which is inscribed in the fleshly tablets of the human heart (Rom 2:15). If, however, I refuse to give an alcoholic the price of a shot of whiskey and feel guilty for not listening to his plea, I experience a measure of neurotic guilt. It is the kind of guilt children experience when they observe their parents drifting apart on the road to divorce, because the children feel it is their fault.

So, likewise, in the question of masturbation, many persons torture themselves needlessly. While it is true that the act of masturbation is *objectively* seriously wrong, it does not follow that the person involved in this act incurs mortal guilt (for example, good-living people who berate themselves about involuntary masturbation). The spiritual counselor or confessor who knows the struggles that persons who suffer from compulsive behavior have had should strive to make it clear that there has been no free consent to the impulse to masturbate.

14.   Is masturbation still gravely sinful, even if there is no free consent?

Objectively, yes. *Subjectively*, however, there is no grievous sin if a person masturbates while lacking in awareness—for example, when he is half-awake, or when he is carried away by sudden passion and finds himself committing the act despite the resistance of his will. This is one of the effects of original sin, i.e., that human passions tend to overcome the acts of the will (Rom 7:15-20). Regarding the subjective guilt of one who commits the sin of masturbation, the *Catechism of the Catholic Church* notes that

> to form an equitable judgment about the subject's moral responsibility and to guide pastoral action, one must take into account the affective immaturity, force of acquired habit, conditions of anxiety, or other psychological or social factors that can lessen, if not even reduce to a minimum, moral culpability.[15]

An individual may agree with this reasoning, yet he may still feel guilty of masturbation in his heart. He may say to himself, "If I had tried harder, I would not have had the fantasies. I should be able to get rid of all my impure thoughts." The trouble with this thought process is that it presupposes that we humans have perfect control over our passions—not only over lust, but also over avarice, anger, and other disordered emotions. Yet we know that we have no such control. The person involved in masturbation, however, needs to believe that with God's grace he can overcome this habit. But it takes faithful adherence to a spiritual program, and, in some cases, psychological counseling as well.

In my pastoral experience, a sense of guilt is the constant companion of masturbation. Many individuals, though, also possess a sense of shame. Whereas guilt involves only the feeling and judgment that one has gone contrary to his conscience and should repent of his wrongdoing, shame is the feeling that "I am no good, I am worthless, and I cannot control my behavior." This intensive self-hatred is at the root of compulsive masturbation, as well as other forms of compulsion. Compulsive masturbation is probably more widespread than any other sexual addiction because it is so accessible and can be indulged in over a long period of time in utter secrecy and *apparently* without harmful social effects.

Tragically, masturbation is a neglected problem in the pastoral ministry of the Church today. The view that it is not a serious problem ignores the data of serious spiritual directors and counselors. Counselors in the areas of drug and sexual addiction insist that their clients seek to get rid of a habit or compulsion which fosters self-indulgence. It is time we confessors and spiritual directors learn from our secular professional colleagues and add to it the wisdom of the teaching of the Church throughout the ages.

15. Could you discuss the connection between pornography and masturbation?

In my pastoral experience, there is a close connection between pornography and masturbation. Both tend to be addictive and both are escapes from reality into fantasy. In some individuals fantasy leads to masturbation, and in other individuals masturbation is the direct consequence of viewing pornography. These two expressions of lust in our culture are serious problems of addiction. Much has been written over the last fifty years on pornography, describing its effects, not only on the individual but also on family, marital relationships, and on other social relationships between man and woman. I desire, however, to study this phenomenon primarily, but not exclusively, in terms of its destructive effects upon individuals. A great number of male adolescents and young college men are snared by Internet pornography, late-night cable television, and pornographic movies.

In working with Courage, I have met some men who have struggled with both masturbation and pornography, and others who have struggled mainly with masturbation. Those who have followed programs like Sexaholics Anonymous have done well, recovering what SA calls one's sexual sobriety.

16. **Has anyone ever written about his or her personal struggles with pornography?**

The following anonymous "psycho-autobiography" will help the reader discern the extent of this evil, not only on the psyche, but also on the soul and body of the individual. I find it necessary to present nearly the entire document. It is a penetrating philosophical analysis by one addicted to pornography.

The Pornographic Self
Anonymous

Why is pornography so powerfully addictive? It can't be because it shows me images of sexual activity... I don't find images of sexual activity in insects, fish, reptiles, or even animals particularly addictive. It is the representation of human sexual activity that is compelling. The first reason for that overwhelming response is the obvious one. I identify. The image representation of sex initiates sexual response in me. I have programmed myself to react to sexual triggers. My own experience of sex has been visual, auditory, tactile, olfactory...The experience of sex, that total body pleasure sensation, is behaviorally associated with sights, sounds, smells, tastes, touches. Any one of these can become the trigger which recalls the entire sex pattern burned into my brain.

There has to be a reason why gynecologists do not have sexual responses when examining patients. They have programmed themselves to examine these organs independently of bodily sexual response...But not me, or the hundreds like me. **My programming deliberately associated images of sexual organs with my own sexual desire.** Now that programming functions automatically, an habitual neural linkage. I am powerless over it. I respond to pornography because I am pornographic.

The power of pornography is really in me, not in the medium... The disturbance that I feel when I encounter sexual representations, the power that I struggle to either deny or enjoy is on the inside. I have created it by conditioning myself to react to triggers. No matter how subtle, a trigger starts a nuclear sex reaction in me which projects sexual fulfillment into my psychic space. I want to participate, to have a sexual experience with the fantasy.... Any representation of available sexual targets is addictive because it nurtures and enhances my conditioning. It increases the mental inventory of my sexual imaging. The addictive appeal is **resident in me, not in the image.**

By focusing the question of power in pornography on what I bring to the image, I discover that there is another reason why pornography is addictive.

Our English word *pornography* comes from a Greek background roughly meaning "selling representations of sex." Written, visual, auditory, or tactile, the concept of the pornographic entails packaging sexual activity in such a way that it can be offered for consumption. Behind the etymology of the word is a second insight into the power of pornography. **It requires deliberate representing or packaging of sexual activity so that a separation occurs between me and the actual human interrelationship of the sexual experience.** For pornography to be successfully tantalizing, it must make me into a voyeur. **Pornography with intimacy is a contradiction in terms.** I believe that this is true because **the pornographic is not about human interrelationship; it is about the myth of the control of intimacy.**

The pornographic representation of sex is a fractured misrepresentation of the only human bodily function which requires interrelationship for completion. The divine character of our humanness can be expressed in the voluntary act of vulnerable self union through sexual encounter with another equally vulnerable human being because this interrelationship brings us close to true selflessness. The demonic distortion of that experience is the fracturing of sex into its mechanical operation and physical organs.

Pornography removes selflessness and human vulnerability from sex. It removes the mystical and mortal by replacing integration with single-self participation. Pornography isolates me from humanness. Real sexual union involves purposeful integration. This is why we distinguish love from sex, even though the two concepts may be fused within the same condition. **Love expresses integration of selves previously separate.** It is the purposeful surrender of self-boundaries in order to include and to yield. It establishes a new joint-self which is essentially an entity separate from either of the two conjoined individuals.

But I cannot find stimulation in pornography unless I disconnect myself from surrender and integration. **Pornography requires dis-integration.** Pornography isolates me from the purposeful integration of sex by reinforcing my psychic and spiritual barriers to vulnerability and mortality. **Pornography offers me the lie of self-protection.** If I have sex with an imaginary person, I cannot be rejected, hurt, abused, debased, shamed, unless I want to be. I am in complete control of the mechanics of my response, and being in control of myself, I come to believe that I can be in complete control of the other. This is why pornography is preoccupied with the fantasy of the possible, denying the reality of the actual. No matter what the medium, pornography demands separation from interrelationship, denying our true communal nature and vulnerability....This prevents confrontation with my real ordinariness, my real inadequacies and my true dependency and finitude. In the process, pornography removes me from any hope of integrity.

All of this separation is also a result of self-programming. Pornography became a tool which I could use to block out the world of hurt and explore the fantasy of pleasure all by myself. **Pornography is not communal. Even when we use it in communal environments** (going to the "adult" theatre, watching a video with someone), its power is always a stimulation of my individual, isolated fantasy. I may act out that fantasy with someone else, but I am not acting in mutual vulnerability. I am simply substituting a live body for an imaginary one. I doubt that pornography would have any appeal at all if it were not essentially about isolation. It was taught to me in isolation. It was explained in isolation.

And my response to it is practiced in isolation. It is powerfully addictive because it focuses my entire psychosomatic spiritual world of that moment on me! It does, practically and spiritually, what I did every time I used a pornographic image—it closes all my doors to the outside world.

This isolation is unbelievably dehumanizing. It is a medium of self-deluded power in a reality of inevitable powerlessness. Sheer humanity reminds us of our mortality. Simply being alive confronts us with our self-delusions of control. Any reasonable introspection causes us to face our inevitable return to the dust from which we came. Our very humanity is the real reason we fear being alive, for the fact of being alive places us in the context of death. And it is death that seems to hold the final card.

Pornography is about the denial of our finitude. It reduces the most intimate human act—an act which cannot be human without vulnerability—to voyeurism, fostering the delusion that life is within my control. In pornography, orgasm proves invulnerability. It convinces me that because I feel the same behavioral results as I would in vulnerable human interrelationship, I can be confirmed as human without the necessary requirement of mutual dependence.

Using pornography deludes me into believing that I am alive because I respond to a representation of the paramount communal act and yet remain invulnerable. The pornographic woman can never hurt me. She can never demand anything of me, spurn me, be ungrateful, inattentive. She can only be used, privately, possessively. The pornographic appeals because it claims to prove that my power of sex overcomes every other one of my failed human efforts to assert my self-identity. **Pornography deliberately intends to drive away death**

through sex. It can only succeed by turning individuals into a demonic lie.

True sexual encounter is the affirmation of individual powerlessness and insignificance precisely because it is about our need to experience love, together, in harmony and vulnerability. **Pornography cannot integrate.** If it did, it would not be pornographic. Its appeal and power resides in the dis-union it produces, the dis-union of witnessing a fantasy of sexual vulnerability without being vulnerable. In the end pornography is manipulative, not because its manufacture requires co-opting the sacred character of sexual intimacy in order to produce the representation of a fractured communal act, but because the representation manipulates me into participation in auto-eroticism. It manipulates me into accepting the lie that sexual activity is the equivalent of human integration. Finally, it manipulates me into believing that sexual activity is only about me—that sex in isolation can restore the imbalance of failure and fear in my soul. The truth is utterly destructive to this lie. **Integration cannot occur without communal interaction and such requires self-surrender.** If sexual union, in representation or participation, does not gather together the separateness of the individuals into a shared entity, then it is pornographic, no matter who is involved. This is why response to pornography is always a version of masturbation, even if it is only mental or a stimulus before intercourse with my spouse. Pornographic response is always only about me. It is sex with myself in an imagined copulation with a fantasy.

Pornography is about sex with alien beings, beings which were once integrated whole persons, but who are now some other form of non-life, moving, breathing, copulating in a world confined to pre-programmed neural passageways. The reason why the cover of

Cosmopolitan is pornographic is not because the model is lascivious. It is because the image is intended to invite anyone and everyone to desire sex with this representation. This is, perhaps, the most damning and the most damaging aspect of pornography. In the final analysis, pornography is not about reality.

Pornography is a perversion of true intimacy just as its representation of sex is a perversion of love. Control is contradictory to the very meaning of intimacy. Intimacy can never be manipulated or controlled. Intimacy is a gift, given only in free interrelationship. Pornography propagates the lie that as I manipulate the image representation of intimacy, I control that intimacy. Every perversion achieves power precisely because it attaches itself to some fractured part of the truth. Pornography is no different. Sex creates. Sex affirms. Pornography pretends creation, affirmation and validation but removes the essential ingredient of a freely given, vulnerable commitment. Pornography pretends to do something that is an oxymoron—it pretends to control intimacy.

In the end I must realize that pornography is addictive and powerful because it is idolatrous. It allows me to go on believing that I am the center of the universe. In fact, its proclivity to isolation not only reinforces my essential idolatry, it literally screams my independence from all community, including the community of God, from every fiber of my being. It uses the most all-encompassing neural, physical, and emotional response to shout in God's face that I do not need him...It seeks to possess (control, manipulate) the object of its desire, even if that object is not the highest possible form of the Beautiful.

Pornography...knows nothing of self-sacrifice based on unmerited, unmotivated giving to another. It knows nothing of denial of self that must result when the wholeness of another is intended. There can be no manipulation or aggrandizement or control of gain exercised when agape is the root of the action, because agape allows for no position for self-love. Pornography is finally about one simple question: God or me?

Notes

1 Benedict Groeshel, C.F.R., *The Courage to Be Chaste* (Mahwah, NJ: Paulist, 1983), pp. 64-65.

2 Joseph Farraher, S.J., "Masturbation," in *New Catholic Encyclopedia* (New York: McGraw-Hill, 1967) vol. 9, pp. 438-440 at 438.

3 The complete text is found in "Letter to a Mr. Masson (March 6, 1956)," Wade Collection, Wheaton College, Wheaton, Illinois.

4 Congregation of the Doctrine of the Faith, *Persona Humana (Declaration on Certain Questions Concerning Sexual Ethics)*, December 29, 1975, no. 9.

5 Farraher, p. 438.

6 William E. May, summary of Silverio Zedda, S.J., *Relativo e assoluto nella morale di San Paolo* (Brescia: Paideia, 1984), p. 393.

7 Ibid. See *Persona Humana*, no. 9.

8 Congregation for Catholic Education, *A Guide to Formation in Priestly Celibacy*, April 11, 1974, no. 63.

9 Patrick Carnes, *Out of the Shadows: Understanding Sexual Addiction*, 3rd ed. (Minneapolis: Hazelden, 2001).

10 John Bradshaw, *Healing the Shame That Binds You* (Deerfield Beach, FL: Health Communications, 1988), pp. 15-19.

11 Patrick Carnes, *The Sexual Addiction* (Minneapolis: CompCare, 1983), p. 4.

12 Rudoph Allers, "Irresistible Impulses, A Question of Moral Philosophy," *American Ecclesiastical Review* 100 (1939): p. 219.

13 Ibid.

14 Ibid., pp. 216-217.

15 *CCC*, no. 2352.

CHAPTER 4

Same-Sex Unions and the Health of Society

Same-sex unions and gay "marriages" have recently become a global issue. Many think such unions are an acceptable alternative to marriage between a man and a woman. Even Catholics often do not know the teaching of the Church on this matter. They do not understand the teaching of both Testaments on the meaning of marriage, nor do they realize that whenever Holy Scripture refers to same-sex sexual acts, it condemns them as immoral.

1. **What is the official teaching of the Catholic Church on same-sex "marriage"?**

On May 2, 2005, a few days after a meeting with Pope Benedict XVI, Cardinal Alfonso Lopez Trujillo, president of the Pontifical Council for the Family, condemned homosexual "marriage" and adoption in an interview with the Fides News Agency. His Eminence said that legislatures which "open the way for same-sex marriage...destroy piece by piece the institution of the family, the most valuable heritage of peoples and humanity." When questioned about allowing same-sex couples to adopt children, he replied: "This would destroy the child's future; it would be an act of moral violence against the child." Later he added, "When he [the child] grows up and becomes an adult, how tragic it will be for him to let his friends know that his 'parents' are two women or two men."[1]

In an address by Pope Benedict XVI to the Ecclesial Congress of the Diocese of Rome in June 2005, the Holy Father referred to the "different present forms of the dissolution of marriage as well as free unions and 'trial marriage,' including the pseudo-marriage between persons of the same sex." The pope added that these forms of marriage are "expressions of an anarchic freedom that appears erroneously as man's authentic liberation."[2]

In short, the Church officially condemns the recent efforts of the legislature in several countries (including several U.S. states) to give legitimacy to so-called "same-sex marriages."

2. Where is the Church's teaching on homosexuality spelled out?

Church teaching on homosexuality and homosexual unions is principally found in three documents from the Congregation for the Doctrine of the Faith (CDF):

- *On the Pastoral Care of Homosexual Persons* (October 1, 1986)

- *On Non-Discrimination against Homosexual Persons: Some Considerations Concerning the Response to Legislative Proposals* (July 23, 1992)

- *Considerations Regarding Proposals to Give Legal Recognition to Unions between Homosexual Persons* (June 3, 2003)

In the first of these documents, *On the Pastoral Care of Homosexual Persons,* the CDF teaches that homosexual acts are, by their very nature, disordered. It also teaches that same-sex attraction (i.e., the inclination to perform same-sex acts), while not a sin in itself, is an objective disorder.

The term used by the Congregation is "intrinsically disordered."[3]

The third document, *Considerations Regarding Proposals to Give Legal Recognition to Unions Between Homosexual Persons,* is concerned with the response of the Catholic Church in particular countries to so-called "gay rights" legislation. It confronts same-sex unions and so-called gay "marriages," and we will examine it in detail to learn what it teaches us about true marriage. It is interesting that the Holy See refuses to use the term "gay marriage" because in no way is a same-sex union a true marriage.

3. **How dangerous would the acceptance of same-sex "marriage" be to the institution of marriage?**

Before proceeding further, we need to put this problem in context. The disintegration of marriage in the United States and throughout Europe has been going on for several decades and has many faces—such as contraception, no-fault divorce, cohabitation, adultery, same-sex unions, and now gay "marriage." Gerard Bradley, professor of law at the University of Notre Dame, states that in comparison with abortion, which is "the greatest injustice in American society...the late twentieth-century disintegration of marriage is more epoch-defining and more hazardous to a persons' moral health. The question of legally recognizing same-sex marriage—thrust upon us by recent court decisions—culminates this disintegration."[4]

4. **Isn't the prohibition of same-sex "marriage" merely a Christian teaching?**

No. This issue relates to the natural moral law, so the CDF's arguments are addressed not only to persons who believe in Christ, but to all persons who care about the common good of society.

What the Church teaches on marriage and the complementarity of the sexes should be clear to human reason. Traditionally defined as one man and one woman coming into a union of one flesh, marriage is recognized by all the major cultures of the world. Marriage is not only a relationship between human beings; it was established by the Creator with its own nature, essential properties, and purposes.[5]

Although it can be blinded by bad philosophy or bad choices, the human spirit naturally knows the truth that marriage exists solely between a man and a woman, joined together in a union of bodily persons expressing their love with the hope of children and family. One does not need texts from Holy Scripture to recognize the institution of marriage and its overriding importance for the common good of the whole human race. Something which is contrary to the natural moral law is *objectively* wrong—regardless of one's particular religious beliefs or opinions.

5.   **What's the problem with the government recognizing same-sex "marriages"? After all, it doesn't arrest people for adultery anymore.**

The duty of government is to protect and defend marriage as an institution essential to the common good. Society owes its continued survival to the family, which is founded on marriage. While it is true that not every immoral act (e.g., adultery) needs to be criminalized, the inevitable result of a *legal* recognition of same-sex unions would be the radical redefinition of marriage. Legally, then, marriage would lose its reference to its essential characteristics—the true union of the spouses and the procreation and education of children.[6] Such a fundamental redefinition of marriage would be gravely detrimental to the common good.

According to St. Thomas Aquinas, "Every humanly created law is legitimate insofar as it is consistent with the natural moral law," which is to say, insofar as it is consistent with moral truths recognized by right reason and respects the inalienable rights of every person.[7] But, as Pope John Paul II points out, "Laws in favor of homosexual unions are contrary to right reason because they confer legal guarantees analogous to those granted in marriage, to unions between persons of the same sex."[8]

For years, society has tolerated private homosexual acts in the same way it has tolerated adultery. But once the state publicly approves this activity, it makes same-sex acts an institution in the legal structure, thus creating a "right" to such acts. This public phenomenon affects the whole of society, particularly the young and their perception and evaluation of forms of behavior. It obscures certain basic moral values, causing a devaluation of the institution of marriage.[9]

6.   **Many same-sex couples say they love each other and only want to show it the way heterosexual couples do. What's wrong with that?**

In sodomy and other forms of homosexual behavior, the joining of the bodies of the persons of the same sex is not such that they are united as persons. Their bodies are reduced to instruments, that is, to each using the other for what they want. In brief, there is no "communion of persons" (*communio personarum*) as there is in marriage. I will develop this and other points associated with your question more fully in the remainder of this chapter.[10]

Same-sex unions are also totally lacking on the conjugal level, which is the human and ordered form of sexuality. Male–female relationships are human to the extent that they promote the complementarity of husband and wife and are open to the transmission of life.[11]

7.   But shouldn't the state recognize that individuals— including homosexuals—have the right to do what they want to do, including to marry?

I refer again to the parameters of authority of the state, which St. Thomas Aquinas makes clear: "Every humanly created law is legitimate insofar as it is consistent with the natural moral law."[12]   The state, if it is to remain responsible for its mandate to govern in accord with the natural moral law, should not establish an institution, such as same-sex "marriage," that is not "consistent with moral truths recognized by right reason."[13]

We can recognize that society owes its own continued survival to the family, founded on marriage. As the CDF puts it, "The inevitable consequence of legal recognition of homosexual unions would be the redefinition of marriage, which would become in its legal status an institution devoid of essential reference to factors linked to heterosexuality; for example, procreation and rearing children."[14]

Today, some invoke the principle of personal autonomy or freedom to justify the legal recognition of homosexual couples. While the civil rights of individuals with same-sex attraction should be affirmed (and indeed are recognized under the U.S. Constitution), there is no reason why same-sex unions should receive special benefits from the state because such unions do not contribute to the common good, as does marriage.

Considerations, by the CDF, points out that "there are good reasons for holding that such unions are harmful to the proper development of human society, especially if their impact on society were to increase."[15] As persons, we live in society and are meant to make a contribution to the common good. Married couples do just that by rearing and educating their children.

Because married couples contribute to the succession of generations by family life, and in this way contribute to the common good of the community, civil law has traditionally granted them institutional recognition. Same-sex couples, however, do not need specific attention from a legal standpoint since they do not exercise this function for the common good.[16]

8. **According to the Church, what does the Bible say about the nature of marriage?**

The CDF holds that there are three fundamental elements in the Creator's plan for marriage, as found in the first two chapters of Genesis.

1. Men and women are equal as persons, and complementary as male and female. "Complementary" means that they are naturally attracted to each other, completing each other on the physical-biological level, and that their sexuality has been raised to a new level—the *personal*, where nature and spirit meet.

2. The Creator instituted marriage as a form of life in which a communion of life is realized, involving the use of the sexual faculty: "Therefore a man leaves his father and mother and cleaves to his wife, and they become one flesh" (Gn 2:24).

3. God has willed to give to the union of man and woman a special share in his work of creation: "Be fruitful and multiply" (Gn 1:28).

9. Does the nature of marriage change in the New Testament?

The beginning of the CDF document deals with Old Testament marriage and natural marriage. But Jesus Himself in the New Testament elevates the institution of marriage to the dignity of a sacrament, and so Christian marriage becomes an efficacious sign of the covenant between Christ and the Church (see Eph 5:32). From this sign come many graces for both husband and wife.[17]

10. Why can't two people of the same sex receive those graces?

Aware of the assumption some make that there are similarities between same-sex unions and true marriage, the CDF responds that there are absolutely "no grounds for considering homosexual unions to be in any way similar, or even remotely analogous to God's plans for marriage and the family." Marriage is holy, while homosexual acts are contrary to the natural moral law. Such acts "close the sexual act to the gift of life. They do not proceed from a genuine affective and sexual complementarity. Under no circumstances can they be approved." Holy Scripture condemns homosexual acts as a "serious depravity."

The CDF is careful to point out that the condemnation of homosexual acts does not mean that "all those who suffer from this anomaly are personally responsible for it, but it does attest to the fact that homosexual acts are intrinsically disordered." This same moral judgment is found in many Christian writers of the first centuries and is unanimously accepted by divine oral tradition. Nevertheless, like other Christians, persons with same-sex tendencies are called to live the virtue of chastity.

11. Why was *Considerations* written?

Considerations is addressed principally to bishops and Catholic politicians in the United States and Canada, where the bishops had accomplished little in battling dissenting homosexual groups. By the time this strong statement of the CDF was published, the movement to legalize same-sex unions had won a position of power in both Canada and the United States.

12. If same-sex unions are so wrong, how did laws permitting them get passed in several countries?

Unfortunately, over the past fifteen years or so, many people, Catholics and non-Catholics alike, did very little to oppose these laws. Thus, legislatures in several countries approved bills which legalized the cohabitation of homosexual persons. We always need to be keep in mind that "the approval or legalization of evil is something different from the toleration of evil."[18] When one *approves* evil, he or she becomes a formal cooperator with evil. However, one may *tolerate* evil when there is no other recourse.

13. What should the response of Catholics be to such laws?

The CDF, in its 2003 document, describes several kinds of situations and the response of Catholics to each. First, in those places where homosexual unions have been legally recognized or have been given the legal status and rights belonging to marriage, "clear and emphatic" opposition is a duty.[19]

"One must refrain from any kind of formal cooperation in the enactment or application of such gravely unjust laws, and, as far as possible, from material cooperation on the level of their application. In this area everyone can exercise the right of conscientious objection."[20] Some justices of the peace in Massachusetts have done this. In addition, a Catholic lawmaker has a duty to express "his opposition clearly and publicly and to vote against it. To vote in favor of a law so harmful to the common good is gravely immoral."[21]

If it is not possible to repeal same-sex legislation, a Catholic legislator should make public his opposition to it. The CDF document also says, "If it is not possible to repeal such a law completely, the Catholic politician, recalling the indications contained in [Pope John Paul II's 1995 encyclical] *Evangelium Vitae,* 'could licitly support proposals aimed at limiting the harm done by such a law and at lessening its negative consequences at the level of general opinion and public morality,' on condition that his 'absolute personal opposition' to such laws was clear and well known and the danger of scandal was avoided."[22]

14. Has Church teaching on homosexuality developed in recent years?

Dr. William E. May, a professor at the John Paul II Institute for Studies in Marriage and the Family, uses a fourth document of the CDF, *Persona Humana* (1975), in addition to the three I have already mentioned. This document clearly distinguishes between the inclination to homosexual acts and the acts themselves, which are always immoral. A subsequent 1986 document, *The Pastoral Care of Homosexual Persons (PCHP)*, is more comprehensive. It corrected mistaken interpretations of the previous document as well as erroneous understandings of Sacred Scripture. The 1975 document left the impression that same-sex attraction is neutral, or even good, but *PCHP* makes it clear that it is an "objective disorder."[23]

Same-sex attraction is called an objective disorder, because if one yields to the inclination, he commits an "intrinsically disordered" act, i.e., an act that is immoral by its very nature. *PCHP* is careful to point out that the inclination is not a sin but "a more or less strong tendency ordered toward an intrinsic moral evil."[24]

15. Aren't we now more knowledgeable about these matters than people in Bible times?

PCHP corrects the view that Scripture is culture-bound, pointing out that there is "a clear consistency within the Scriptures themselves on the moral issue of homosexual behavior." The Church's teaching is based on the solid foundation of a constant biblical testimony.

May stresses the truth that arguments from Holy Scripture must be joined with arguments from Sacred Tradition, as

stated in *Dei Verbum*, Vatican II's Dogmatic Constitution
on Divine Revelation, which affirms that Tradition, Sacred
Scripture, and the teaching authority of the Church (the
Magisterium) are "so connected and associated that one
of them cannot stand without the others."[25] This is a
key principle to interpreting the Scriptures in Catholic
theology, since from the beginning the Magisterium has
interpreted the Scriptures within the tradition of the
Church.

PCHP "affirms that the Church's teaching on homosexual
acts is rooted in God's plan concerning the life-giving and
loving union of man and woman in marriage."[26] It is only in
the marital relationship that sexual intercourse is morally
good. From this it follows that in choosing someone of the
same sex, one annuls the rich symbolism and meaning as
well as the goals of God's plan for the union of man and
woman in marriage. Homosexual activity does not involve
complementarity, it is not able to transmit life, and so it
thwarts the call to a life of self-giving, which the Gospel
says is the fullness of Christian living. Again, like every
moral disorder, homosexual activity frustrates one's own
fulfillment because it is acting contrary to the creative
wisdom of God.[27]

16. **But don't homosexuals have to act out this way? After
    all, that's why they're called "homosexuals."**

PCHP rejects this argument given to justify homosexual
acts, i.e., that persons with same-sex attraction have no
other choice than to act in a homosexual way because of
their lack of freedom. *PCHP* rejects this argument because
it is rooted in the "unfounded and demeaning assumption
that the sexual behavior of homosexual persons is always
and totally compulsive and therefore inculpable."[28]

In section twelve of *PCHP*, individuals with same-sex attraction are called to join their difficulties in living a chaste life to the cross of Jesus Christ. Self-denial is not pointless: "The cross *is* a denial of self, but in the service to the will of God himself, who makes life come from death and empowers those who trust in him to practice virtue in place of vice."[29] We will examine more about this in a later chapter.

17. Why are homosexual acts always gravely immoral?

William May argues from the statement of John Paul II "that the commandments of which Jesus reminds the young man (see Mt 19:16-30; Mk 10:17-22; Lk 18:18-30) are meant to safeguard the *good* of the person, the image of God, by protecting his *goods*."[30] From this, May draws the conclusion that if homosexual acts are gravely immoral, they are so because they harm the goods of human persons. The goods harmed by such acts are the goods of marriage and of the body's capacity for the marital act as an act of self-giving, which constitutes a communion of bodily persons—which John Paul II calls the "nuptial meaning of the body."[31]

May holds that it is necessary to show that the marriage of a man and woman is *intrinsically* good (i.e., good in and of itself) and not merely *instrumentally* good (i.e., not something that merely serves to achieve another good), and that the marital act in which they give themselves to each other honors this good and the "nuptial meaning of the body." This is a very important point, which has been made by professors John Finnis of Oxford University, Germain Grisez of Mount St. Mary's College, and others.[32]

The notion that marriage is a basic good is central to the teaching of John Paul II. In his 1981 apostolic exhortation on the family, *Familiaris Consortio*, he identifies marriage as one way of realizing the human vocation to love.[33] In *Mulieris Dignitatem* (1988), the Holy Father declares that the communion of persons *(communio personarum)* of husband and wife is an image of the Trinity's own communion of persons.[34] In addition, his 1993 encyclical *Veritatis Splendor* explicitly refers to the communion of persons in marriage as a fundamental human good.[35]

May points out that the unmarried may be capable of genital acts, but not of marital acts,

> precisely because they are not married, and it is marriage that capacitates spouses to engage in the marital act, i.e., to do what spouses are supposed to do, to become literally one flesh in an act whereby the man personally *gives* himself to his wife by entering into her body person, and by doing so *receives* her, and whereby the woman personally *receives* her husband into her body person, and by doing so *gives* herself to him in a receiving way...The conjugal or marital act actually unites two persons who have made each other irreplaceable, non-substitutable, and non-disposable in their lives by *giving* themselves to one another, and *receiving* one another in marriage.[36]

18. But couldn't homosexual acts be likened to sex between an infertile married couple?

No. Marriage is an intrinsic or basic human good, and as such "provides a non-instrumental reason for spouses to engage in the marital act"[37]; that is, a couple does not have sexual intercourse for some reason other than the fact that they are married. From this truth, William May draws the conclusion that the marital act "remains a *procreative* or *reproductive* kind of act even if the spouses, because of non-behavioral factors over which they have no control, for example, the temporary or permanent sterility of one of the spouses, are not able to generate human life in a freely chosen marital act."[38] Their act remains "the kind of bodily act which alone is 'apt' for generating human life," which homosexual sex cannot do.

Regarding sex in an infertile marriage, May quotes Princeton University professor Robert George and Notre Dame Law School professor Gerard Bradley, who state that "the intrinsic point of sex in marriage, fertile or not, is...the basic good of marriage itself, considered as a two-in-one-flesh communion of persons that is consummated and actualized by acts of the reproductive type."[39]

Pope John Paul II has written perceptively of the "language of the body" and the way in which the marital act speaks this language. May points to a summary of the pope's thought in *Donum Vitae (Respect for Human Life in its Origins and on the Dignity of Human Procreation)*, a 1987 CDF instruction: "Spouses mutually express their personal love in the 'language of the body,' which clearly involves both 'spousal meanings' and parental ones...It is an act that is inseparably corporal and spiritual. It is in their bodies and through their bodies that the spouses consummate their marriage, and are able to become father and mother."[40]

John Finnis, likewise, speaks of the spouses as one reality who, by their sexual union, can *actualize* and allow them to *experience* their real common good—*their marriage with the two goods* of parenthood and friendship.[41]

In the answer to question seventeen, May demonstrated that marriage is an intrinsic, fundamental human good which is exercised through the two-in-one-flesh union of husband and wife. In the answer to the next question (nineteen), May shows how homosexual acts damage the goods of marriage and of the nuptial meaning of the body. May believes that couples with same-sex attraction can live in a committed relationship with mutual affection expressed in a chaste way. This is a form of friendship which happens among older persons who have practiced chastity for a considerable period of time. It is comparatively rare, and such a relationship needs spiritual monitoring. Actually, many members of Courage remain chaste, while avoiding committed friendships and preferring to be part of a group of friends.

Usually, however, persons with same-sex attraction who make a commitment to one another have an active sex life. Inasmuch as these same-sex couples form an economic unit, they have a just claim to benefits that can be granted to other same-sex couples living together, for instance, widows or widowers. Homosexual couples might claim that they cannot satisfy their sexual urges and inclinations toward intimate union in any more adequate way than "by establishing a more or less permanent relationship that includes sexual intimacy, and that one appropriate way for them to express their affection and friendship is to engage in homosexual acts."[42] After presenting a homosexual view of an appropriate act of affection, May asks whether these acts are truly appropriate to express affection.

19. So what is the moral object of homosexual acts?

To answer this question, May uses the argument of Patrick Lee, a professor at Franciscan University of Steubenville, and Robert George of Princeton University. They make clear that when one chooses to actualize one's bodily, sexual power as an extrinsic means of producing an effect in one's consciousness, then one separates in one's choice *oneself as bodily from oneself as an intentional agent*. One reduces one's bodily self to the level of an *extrinsic* instrument, bringing about a dis-integration of self. But when one treats one's body as *intrinsic* to one's self, there is a unitary activity, and various bodily actions share in that activity since they are not directed to an extrinsic purpose.[43]

In other words, when someone chooses to use his sexual powers merely to experience pleasure, he is using his body as an instrument, as a means to an end. The complete person, on the other hand, treats his body as an integral part of himself.

In unitary activity, one freely chooses real goods, such as the good of play in basketball, or the good of health in exercising, or the good of friendship in writing a letter or in conversing, and one's efforts in realizing these goods involve, where appropriate, one's bodily activity. So, likewise, in the marital act spouses freely choose to make their communion of persons in one flesh open to the gift of life in and through an act in which their *bodily activity* is as much the constitutive subject of what they are doing as is their act of choice.[44]

20. But aren't same-sex couples being intimate when they engage in such acts? Isn't that a good?

While they may use these acts, according to Finnis, as a "means of experiencing personal intimacy, the resulting experience cannot be the experience of any real unity between them."[45] Indeed, Grisez has put it so accurately:

[E]ach one's experience of intimacy is private and incommunicable, and no more a common good than is the mere experience of sexual arousal and orgasm. Therefore, the choice to engage in sodomy for the sake of that experience of intimacy in no way contributes to the partners' real common good as committed friends.[46]

Thus persons choosing homosexual acts decide to use their own, and each others' bodies to get subjective satisfactions, or states of consciousness. In this way the body becomes an instrument used, and the conscious subject the user. The conscious self is alienated from the body, resulting in an existential dualism between the body and the conscious subject, i.e. 'a division between the two insofar as they are co-principles of oneself considered as an integrated, acting, sexual person.[47]

To choose to engage in homosexual acts is to choose a specific kind of disintegration, whereas the human person requires integration in order to be fulfilled. As Grisez continues, "this specific act of self integration...is precisely the aspect necessary so that the bodily union of sexual intercourse will be a communion of persons, as marital intercourse is."[48] Therefore, homosexual acts *damage* the body's capacity for the marital act as an act of self-giving, which constitutes a communion of bodily persons, or, in other words, "the nuptial meaning of the body."

21. Can you explain more about the "nuptial meaning of the body" and how this relates to homosexual acts?

From the arguments of Lee, George, and Grisez, May draws the conclusion that homosexual acts damage the good of the body's capacity for self-gift, its nuptial meaning.

[Homosexual] acts, moreover, are ones in which those engaging in them do not even encounter each other face to face, a uniquely *human* way of copulating, but rather in a way characteristic of sub-human animals...Inasmuch as homosexual acts damage the nuptial meaning of the body, they also damage the good of marriage itself. They do so because the great good of marriage requires that spouses recognize that their bodies are integral to their being as persons, and that it is precisely their sexual complementarity, revealed in their bodily differences, that makes it possible for the man to 'give himself in a receiving way' to his wife in the marital act, and for his wife 'to receive him in a giving way' in this same act, an act having two common subjects.[49]

22. So, bottom line, there can't be same-sex marriages, right?

May answers this question in this way: "Persons of the same sex cannot marry, because they cannot do what married couples can do, i.e., to consummate their union by a bodily act in which they become the common subjects of an act that, precisely as human behavior, is eminently fit both for the communication of spousal love and for the generation of new human life."[50]

The spousal union goes beyond the biological union, but biology is an essential component. By their marital acts husband and wife express in a profound way their own married life together: two in one flesh. It is noted that genital intercourse is the *only* bodily act intrinsically capable of generating new human life. Other forms of expressing affection cannot generate children. Although they may be generated through acts of fornication and adultery, it is not good for children to be born in this way. From the beginning of human culture every generation has perceived the bond linking sex, marriage, and the generation of human life, and has frowned upon begetting children out of wedlock.

Our society, like any other society, can survive only if new human persons are generated. The marital union of a man and a woman who have given themselves unreservedly in marriage "is the best place to serve as a 'home' for new human life, as the 'place' where this life can take root and grow in love and service to others. Such marriages contribute uniquely to the common good, and they merit legal protection. Same-sex unions are not the same, sadly mimicking the real thing. In no way can they be regarded as true marriages."[51]

23. What about same-sex couples adopting children?

Considerations, the June 2003 document of the Congregation for the Doctrine of the Faith, clearly states that homosexual adoption does violence to the child, who is deprived of the experience of normal development in an intact marriage of man and woman as mother and father.[52] This position is supported by Maggie Gallagher and Joshua K. Baker in their article, "Do Moms and Dads Matter? Evidence from the Social Sciences on Family Structure and the Best Interests of the Child."[53] Gallagher and Baker point out that in the last thirty years "literally tens of thousands of studies evaluating the consequences of marriage have been conducted in various disciplines...As a group, these studies point to powerful advantages of intact marriages of a mother and a father for children."[54]

Gallagher and Baker speak of an emerging consensus among social scientists on the importance of family structure for child well-being. They quote the summary of twelve leading family scholars: "Marriage is an important social good associated with an impressively broad array of positive outcomes for children and adults alike...Whether American society succeeds or fails in building a healthy marriage culture is clearly a matter of legitimate public concern."[55] These scholars hold that it is important that American society builds a healthy marriage culture. They also come to twelve conclusions about family structure, all of which presuppose that the best interests of children are protected by an intact marriage of man and woman.[56]

> Marriage is more than a private emotional relationship. It is also a social good. Not every person can or should marry. And not every child raised outside of marriage is damaged as a result. But communities where good enough marriages are common have better outcomes for children, women, and men than do communities suffering from high rates of divorce, unmarried childbearing, and high conflict or violent marriages.[57]

In more recent times, this scholarly consensus on the importance of marriage for childbearing has deepened to become the conventional wisdom among mainstream child-welfare organizations. For example, a *Child Trends* research brief summed up the scholarly consensus: "Research clearly demonstrates that family structure matters for children, and the family structure that helps the most is a family headed by two biological parents in a low conflict marriage."[58] An Urban Institute scholar concluded: "Even among the poor, material hardships were substantially lower among married couples with children than with other families with children."[59]

Furthermore, a report from the Centers for Disease Control and Prevention (CDC) and another from the Center for Law and Social Policy reaffirm the proposition that children benefit most from two biological parents in an intact marriage.[60]

The reader can find the important details of the arguments of Gallagher and Baker in opposition to other views on the Courage website.[61]

24. Can you sum up the Church's moral teaching, then, on this issue?

Having carefully studied the arguments of Patrick Lee, Robert George, John Finnis, Germain Grisez, and William E. May, I see a twofold conclusion:

1. Those performing homosexual acts are using their bodies and the bodies of other persons as mere instruments of their lust, and rendering themselves incapable of the marital act.

2. Only a man and a woman married to one another are capable of a one-flesh union, a union with two subjects in the fullness of their body-soul persons. Those engaged in homosexual acts are in a process of dis-integration, making themselves incapable of giving oneself as a whole person to someone of the other sex.

In addition, *Considerations* is opposed to children being raised by same-sex couples.

25. What is happening legally with same-sex "marriage"?

In state referenda during the 2004 elections, eleven states voted in favor of bans against same-sex "marriage." Throughout the country since 1996, state legislators have been busy drafting defense-of-marriage acts. The Supreme Judicial Court of Massachusetts commanded the state legislature to legalize same-sex marriages, and it was done. This is a form of judicial despotism.

Other states are very concerned that they may be forced to recognize such marriages, because of the "full faith and credit clause" in the U.S. Constitution that marriage laws in one state be accepted in all other states. There seems to be a race between the courts and legislatures to define marriage. Court decisions in favor of same-sex marriage have led to campaigns to nullify those decisions by passing constitutional amendments to define marriage as the union of one man and one woman. As of June 1, 2007, fourteen states already have laws which define marriage as requiring one man and one woman, and initiatives for state constitutional amendments have been successful in twenty-seven states.[62] Numerous other challenges to the status quo have arisen in Canada and Europe, all of which are in varying stages of litigation.

26. How have Christians responded to the challenge of same-sex marriage?

People of faith have perceived that the institution of marriage is in jeopardy and that they need to become involved in the public square. We can see this in the results of the 2004 elections: All eleven states that gave their citizens a chance to vote on constitutional amendments defining marriage as the union between one man and one woman won their initiatives overwhelmingly. Arkansas, Georgia, Kentucky, Michigan, Mississippi, Montana, North Dakota, Ohio, Oklahoma, Oregon, and Utah won decisive victories for the Alliance for Marriage Campaign. Robert Knight of the Alliance for Marriage commented on this groundswell for the Defense of Marriage Act: "There is absolutely no question as to where Americans stand on this issue....The eleven states with amendments on the ballot represent diverse populations that have come together to defend marriage."[63]

While we may rejoice that the issue of "gay marriage" induced so many voters to make "moral values" their primary motive for voting, still we should not rest because the struggle between legislators and activist judges will continue on this issue. As citizens of America and as people of faith, we must work for the preservation of laws that affirm the permanent and exclusive union of one man and one woman.

Notre Dame law professor Gerard Bradley has some pertinent observations on the legal aspects of same-sex unions. As a result of a Vermont Supreme Court decision, *Baker v. State*, the state legislature conferred upon same-sex couples all the benefits of marriage except the *status* of marriage. Since then Massachusetts' highest court has taken the next step: no discrimination whatsoever in marriage law on the basis of the genders of a couple seeking to marry. The question has already arisen: Will these same-sex "marriages" be recognized in other states to which Massachusetts couples travel or relocate, as are heterosexual marriages? This is the "full faith and credit" question, and it is one way in which judicial activism could force same-sex "marriage" upon the whole country.

Professor Bradley challenges the Congress of the United States to develop a federal amendment in defense of marriage before the current Supreme Court approves same-sex marriages. This is one more reason to struggle for a federal amendment to the Constitution, affirming that marriage is a permanent and exclusive union between one man and one woman.

27. Since the battle over same-sex marriage has shifted to the courts, what has the U.S. Supreme Court said about marriage in the past?

Notre Dame's Gerard Bradley gives two examples of the long, traditional judicial testimony concerning the institution of marriage. He cites *Maynard v. Hill*, wherein the U.S. Supreme Court said that "marriage creates 'the most important relation in life' and has more to do with the morals and civilization of a people than any other institution. Marriage, also, the Court said, 'is the foundation of the family and of society, without which there would be neither civilization nor progress.'"[64] In 1961, Justice Harlan said:

> The very inclusion of the category of morality among state concerns indicates that society is not limited in its objects only to the physical well-being of the community, but has traditionally concerned itself with the moral soundness of the people as well.[65]

Harlan goes on to say that sexual-genital relationships must be confined to the institution of marriage.[66]

28. Why has the law traditionally considered marriage as supporting the "common good" of society?

According to Gerard Bradley, there are two features of marriage which legislators from time immemorial have selected

> out of the complex open-ended relationship as *critically* important to the political common good: marriage as the principle of sexual morality, and marriage as the only legitimate setting in which children should come to be, and be raised. It has surely been the undoing of marriage that, as a society, we have detached both sex and marriage from children.[67]

Bradley believes that many people do not understand the traditional thinking that marriage is

> a one-flesh communion of persons consummated and actualized in the reproductive-type acts of spouses...For this reason whatever undermines the sound understanding and practice of marriage in a culture—including ideologies that are hostile

to that understanding and practice—makes it difficult for
people to grasp the intrinsic value of marriage and marital
intercourse.[68]

Longstanding legal and religious traditions "testify to
the intrinsic value of marriage as a two-in-one-flesh
communion." If either the husband or the wife is not able to
consummate the marriage, then there is no marriage. The
law concerning the necessity of consummation "embodies
an important insight into the nature of marriage as a
bodily—no less than spiritual and emotional—union that
is actualized in reproductive-type acts."[69]

Proponents of same-sex marriage are not willing to admit
that intercourse between husband and wife is necessary for
marriage, believing that anal and oral intercourse between
same-sex persons constitutes an emotional union. Most
people, however, perceive the special meaning of the genital
intercourse of spouses, even if they are incapable of having
children, or any more children. Their common sense tells
them that couples of the same sex are not capable of
marriage.

In the view of people of faith, "children conceived in
marital intercourse participate in the good of their
parents' marriage and are themselves non-instrumental
aspects of their perfection: thus, spouses rightly hope for
and welcome children, not as 'products' they 'make' but
rather as gifts...This understanding of children as gifts to
be accepted and valued for their own sake—rather than as
objects, that may be willed and brought into being for one's
own purposes" resonates particularly with Christians and
Jews. From the moral relationship of parents to children
comes an affirmation of the dignity of children "as *persons*,
i.e. as *ends in themselves*, and not mere *means* of satisfying

desires of their parents: as *subjects* of justice...rather than objects of will."[70]

29. What about the question of civil rights, though? Homosexuals claim their rights won't be guaranteed until they are granted the right of "marriage."

Bradley holds that "homosexuality is irrelevant to almost every question pertaining to the common good of political society. This is partly because the most important human rights are civil rights. Human rights attach to everyone because they are human persons."[71] Sexual orientation, however, does not change the reality of human rights.

Bradley lists other reasons why homosexuality is "almost entirely irrelevant":

1. People are to be judged on the basis of their conduct, not their inclinations. One is not punished for having same-sex attraction.

2. Most of the particular rights and duties of civil and political life do not "implicate one's sexual activity, habits, or orientation—whatever they may be."

3. A person with same-sex attraction can form good friendships and reduce loneliness in his life, as so many members of Courage have experienced.

30. Where is the law headed on this issue?

Writing in 2004, Judge Robert H. Bork stated his opinion that the current Supreme Court's "ongoing campaign to normalize homosexuality—creating for homosexuals constitutional rights to special voting status and to engage in sodomy—leaves little doubt that the Court has set its course for a right to marry."[72]

This is but one case of the relentless movements to do away with the institution of marriage and the rule of law in constitutional interpretation. Such judicial action has already blurred the lines between objective norms of right and wrong and the opinion of the individual who, having lost sight of objective norms, has become a slave of his own desires. Bork refers to what is now known as the "mystery passage," found in the majority opinion of the Supreme Court's 2003 decision *Lawrence v. Texas,* which created a right to homosexual sodomy. Three Justices stated that our laws provided constitutional protection to individuals to make choices in accord with their desires; at the heart of their personal liberty "is the right to define one's own concept of existence, of meaning, of the universe, and of the mystery of human life."

"The above decision of the Supreme Court," Judge Bork says, "gives each person the right to make up his own law. This is anarchy." The only real hope of heading off the judicial drive to constitutionalize homosexual "marriage" is the adoption of an amendment to the Constitution.

31. Hasn't an amendment to forbid same-sex marriage been proposed?

Yes. The Federal Marriage Amendment (FMA) to the United States Constitution has been proposed. This amendment would define marriage in the United States as the union of one man and one woman and would also prevent judicial extension of marriage-like rights to same-sex or other unmarried couples, as well as preventing people from having multiple spouses. In the most recent vote, which took place in the U.S. Senate on June 7, 2006, the proposed amendment failed to pass. Forty-nine senators voted for putting the amendment to vote, while forty-eight voted against, thus falling short of the two-thirds necessary for passage.

The language of the amendment states that "marriage in the United States shall consist only of the union of a man and a woman. Neither this constitution, nor the constitution of any state shall be construed to require that the marital status, or the legal incidents thereof be conferred upon unmarried couples or groups."[73]

Such language is meant to stop activist courts from redefining marriage in the way that the Supreme Judicial Court of Massachusetts has done. It is probable that the battle to support and preserve traditional marriage by means of a federal amendment to the Constitution will be very difficult. As Judge Bork observes, "[The situation] is made immeasurably more difficult because so many people ask: How does homosexual marriage affect me? What concern is it of mine, or of anyone else what homosexuals do? The answer is that the consequences of homosexual marriage will affect you, your children, and your grandchildren, as well as the morality and health of the society in which you and they live."[74]

Like Gerard Bradley and Kenneth Whitehead, Bork points out that such unions will lead to a complete breakdown of moral standards in human sexual activity. "With same-sex marriage a line is being crossed, and no other line to separate moral and immoral consensual sex will hold."[75]

Bork also asks whether passing a federal amendment is worth the battle to politicians when there is a good chance of losing. He responds that "this issue is so important that a fight against it, whatever the odds, is mandatory."[76] Bork warns religious leaders that there will be no immunities for them or the faithful laity. Without doubt, the Catholic Church will be attacked.

Like Bradley, Bork fears that if our political leaders wait until the Supreme Court imposes same-sex marriage upon our nation, it may be too late for an effective response. At present, we may be pessimistic that Congress will act to move forward with a constitutional amendment yet hopeful that religious leaders and the general public will publicly affirm traditional marriage and family life.

32. What else can we do to prevent the legalization of "gay marriage"?

Christian people need to work to reform the basic attitudes of Americans concerning the nature of marriage, the meaning of chastity, the rights of children, the no-fault divorce game, and the support of family life as a step in the right direction for the continuation of traditional marriage. We need to oppose the use of contraceptives and abortion in every way possible. We should become involved in the political process. As of this writing (June 2007) I favor a constitutional amendment, but it may be that by the time this book is printed, the text of the then current amendment may be something quite different than now, and maybe something not desirable at all.

We need to be clear that the traditional law concerning marriage has seen it as the exclusive union of one man and one woman, and this law must be preserved. Marriage deeply affects our culture and our code of sexual morality. For more than thirty years, the Church has supported crusades of prayer to bring an end to legalized abortion. Now we need constant prayers to the Sacred Heart for the institution of marriage, that it may be strengthened by the laws of every state. This will not be easy, as I have learned in observing the power of the gay movement in the United States, Canada, Spain, and other countries.

33. But can the current movement in society toward "gay marriage" be effectively opposed?

Yes, but only with difficulty and much prayer. In my book *The Truth about Homosexuality* I traced the growth of the gay movement over several decades. It is now a tremendously powerful force throughout the world, discouraging chastity as outmoded. It threatens freedom of religion because it is a direct attack upon our culture, marriage, and our faith. For many years I have spoken out against the gay movement to Catholic audiences throughout the world. But it is very difficult to wake up our Catholic people. They fail to see that this is a cultural and religious battle. Will our country wake up before it is too late? As Midge Decter has said, "We are given the choice of leaving (our young people) with a blessing or a curse."[77]

Notes

1   *The Wanderer*, May 12, 2005, pp. 1-2.

2   Zenit News Agency, "Benedict XVI on Anthropological Foundation of the Family" (Part 1). Zenit.org, June 9, 2005, http://www.zenit.org/article-13255?l=english. Part 2 can be found at http://www.zenit.org/article-13265?l=english.

3   *On the Pastoral Care of Homosexual Persons (PCHP)*, no. 3.

4   Gerard Bradley, "Same-Sex Marriage: The End of Marriage?" *Catholic Dossier*, March-April 2001, p. 36.

5   See *CCC*, no. 1603; *Gaudium et Spes*, no. 48.

6   See *CCC*, no. 1601; *Code of Canon Law*, no. 1055.

7   Thomas Aquinas, *Summa Theologiae*, I-II, 95, 2.

8   John Paul II, *Evangelium Vitae* (1995), no. 90.

9   See *Considerations Regarding Proposals to Give Legal Recognition to Unions Between Homosexual Persons, no.* 5.

10   The answers to questions twenty through twenty-two, for example, speak of the disintegration that same-sex acts introduce into the personalities involved in them.

11   *Considerations*, 7.

12   Aquinas, *Summa Theologiae*, I-II, 95, 2. See answer to question five, above.

13   Ibid.

14   *Considerations*, no. 8.

15   Ibid.

16   See *Considerations*, no. 9.

17   *Considerations*, no 3.

18   Ibid., no. 5.

¹⁹ Ibid. "Where the government's policy is *de facto* tolerance and there is no explicit recognition of homosexual unions, it is necessary to distinguish carefully the various aspects of the problem. Moral conscience requires that on every occasion Christians give witness to the whole moral truth, which is contradicted both by approval of homosexual acts and unjust discrimination against homosexual persons. Therefore, discreet and prudent actions can be effective; these might involve: unmasking the way in which such tolerance might be exploited or used in the service of ideology; stating clearly the immoral nature of these unions; reminding the government of the need to contain the phenomenon within certain limits so as to safeguard public morality and, above all, to avoid exposing young people to erroneous ideas about sexuality and marriage that would deprive them of the necessary defenses and contribute to the spread of the phenomenon" (*Considerations*, no. 5).

²⁰ Ibid.

²¹ Ibid.

²² *Evangelium Vitae*, no. 90.

²³ *On the Pastoral Care of Homosexual Persons (PCHP)*, no. 3.

²⁴ Ibid.

²⁵ *Dei Verbum*, no. 10.

²⁶ *PCHP*, no. 7.

²⁷ See ibid.

²⁸ *PCHP*, no. 11. See May's commentary on this section in "On the Impossibility of Same-Sex Marriage," *The National Catholic Bioethics Quarterly* 4, no. 2 (Summer 2004): 307.

²⁹ *PCHP*, no. 12. In his commentary ("Impossibility," p. 307) May also mentions the foundation of Courage as a support system to help persons with same-sex attraction to be chaste.

³⁰ *Veritatis Splendor*, no. 13.

³¹ May, "Impossibility," p. 310; May's commentary on *Veritatis Splendor*, no. 13.

³² Ibid.

33 *Familiaris Consortio*, no. 11.

34 *Mulieris Dignitatem*, no. 7.

35 *Veritatis Splendor*, no. 13.

36 May, "Impossibility," p. 312. May refers to "Marriage and the Liberal Imagination" by Robert P. George and Gerard V. Bradley, in *Georgetown Law Journal* 84 (1995): pp. 301-302.

37 Ibid., p. 311.

38 Ibid.

39 Ibid., p. 312. May quoting Robert George and Gerard Bradley.

40 Ibid., p. 313. May quoting John Paul II on the language of the body with its spousal and parental meanings.

41 Ibid., p.313. See John Finnis, "Law, Morality, and 'Sexual Orientation,'" *Notre Dame Law Review* 69 (1994): p. 1066.

42 Ibid. p. 313. May quotes Steven Macedo, "Sexuality and Liberty," from *Sex, Preference and Family*, ed. Estlund and Nussbaum (New York: Oxford University Press, 1977), pp. 90-97.

43 May, "Impossibility," p. 315.

44 Ibid. May references Patrick Lee and Robert George's point that using the sexual powers as a mere instrument leads to a split between the intentional agent and the body.

45 Ibid. May points out that homosexual acts do not lead to a true unity of two body persons.

46 Ibid. May quotes Grisez, who holds that the choice to engage in sodomy does not contribute to the partners' real common good.

47 Ibid. May quotes Grisez speaking of the division between the conscious self and the body.

48 Ibid.

49 Ibid., p. 316.

50 Ibid. May holds that same-sex acts make marriage between such persons impossible.

51 Ibid. May concludes that a marriage can only be between a man and a woman.

52   *Considerations,* no. 7.

53   Published in *Margins: Maryland's Law Journal on Race, Religion, Gender and Class* 4 (2004), pp. 161-80.

54   Ibid., p. 165.

55   Ibid., p. 161.

56   Ibid., p.163.

57   Ibid., p.164. Quoted by Gallagher-Baker.

58   Ibid., p.165. Quoted by G-B.

59   Ibid., nn, 18, 19. Quoted by G-B.

60   Ibid., n. 20.

61   This will be placed on the Courage website, www.couragerc.org, in October 2007.

62   See Gerard V. Bradley and William L. Saunders, Jr., "DOMA Won't Do It: Why the Constitution Must be Amended to Save Marriage." Family Research Council, http://www.frc.org/get.cfm?i=BC04D03.

63   Jody Brown and Allie Martin, "Traditional Marriage Exalted in Every State's Amendment Vote," *Agape Press,* Nov. 3, 2004.

64   Gerard V. Bradley, "Same-Sex Marriage: Our Final Answer?" in *Same-Sex Attraction: A Parents' Guide,* ed. John F. Harvey, O.S.F.S. and Gerard V. Bradley (South Bend, IN: St. Augustine's Press, 2003), p. 137.

65   Ibid., pp. 137-38. Bradley quotes Harlan.

66   Ibid., p. 138.

67   Ibid.

68   Ibid.

69   Ibid., p. 139.

70   Ibid.. See also May, pp. 313-16.

71   Bradley, p. 141.

72   Robert H. Bork, "The Necessary Amendment," *First Things,* August–September 2004, pp. 17-21 at 17. All subsequent quotations in this answer are likewise from this article.

73 Ibid., p. 17.

74 Ibid., p. 19.

75 Ibid., p. 20.

76 Ibid.

77 Midge Decter, "Civil Unions: Compromise or Surrender?" in *Imprimis*, the monthly journal of Hillsdale College, November 2004, p. 7.

CHAPTER 5

Chastity

1. What exactly is chastity?

The moral virtue of chastity is a power pertaining to the sexual appetite by which sexual desires habitually move in accordance with the judgment of reason and the choice of the will.[1]

Chastity is a virtue that is traditionally classified as a form of temperance or moderation with regard to sexual pleasure. The human passions are disordered and difficult to control as a result of original sin. St. Thomas Aquinas explains that the term "chastity" comes "from the fact that reason *chastises* concupiscence, which, like a child, needs curbing."[2]

2. How would you describe the current attitude toward chastity in the United States?

Many Americans believe that chastity is impossible. This is especially true among teenagers. In many contemporary movies, books, and television shows, young people are told that one must have sex in order to be "normal." If one were to take a survey of a group of teenagers—whether at a public or Catholic high school—we would hear that young people regard chastity as either outmoded or too difficult to live out. (Many may not have even heard the word "chastity," much less understand what it means.) How else can one explain the current practice of public schools handing out condoms to students for "safe sex" or groups of high school or college students having wild parties? Young people think this is the normal way to act. Is the message that they do not know any better, or that they know that what they are doing is immoral but cannot control themselves? Or maybe that they do not *want* to control themselves?

I believe most young people know that they are doing something sinful but think that they are unable to control themselves due to peer pressure, the lack of good example from their elders, and the decadent culture in which they live. All this adds up to a kind of despair about their ability to be chaste.

3. Aren't most Catholic teenagers and young adults trying to live chastely?

Even in a Catholic college or university, where many of the students do strive to be chaste, we encounter the phenomenon of "white-knuckled chastity." This is the attitude that chastity is a burden. A young person says, "I know I must be chaste if I want to avoid hell, but it is very difficult because I am strongly attracted by sexual fantasies. I try so hard to get rid of them, but they keep coming back, and often I finally give in to them."

The first thing a young person needs to do is to realize that human sexuality is a gift of God, to appreciate that sexuality in marriage is very good because it comes from God. We must also realize that, as a result of original sin, we are tempted to violate the laws of God with regard to sexual activity. We must not blame our bodies, because lust begins in the desires of the heart. The human body is joined in an intimate union with the human soul. During this life, the body is as much a part of the person as the soul. That is why we use the term "body person."

The intellectual acceptance of the goodness of sexuality, however, is not enough; the emotions under the control of the will must enter into the unified action of the whole person. In the gospel of Matthew, a scribe asks Jesus which of the commandments of the Law is the greatest. Jesus replies: "You shall love the Lord your God with all your heart, with all your soul, and with all your mind" (Mt 22:36-38).

One important step on the way to chastity is the practice of the virtue of continence. I also sometimes refer to this as "white-knuckled chastity" because of the effort involved. In continence the sexual desires put up a strong fight against the command of the will, but if the person keeps fighting, the battle to remain chaste will be won. Continence paves the way for the virtue of chastity.

Prayer enables one to use God's gift of sexuality in the way that He wills it to be used. Through prayer one begins to understand God's plan for human sexuality and therefore desires to be chaste. In other words, one becomes chaste, primarily because he loves Jesus Christ. He puts the love of Christ before every other love. When he is tempted to an impure act with another person or by himself, he remembers that Christ comes first, and he is able to resist the temptation. From pastoral experience I know this to be true, because in the midst of temptation recalling the presence of Christ will help avoid sin.

4. Besides prayer, what can a person do to live chastely?

Another aid to the practice of chastity is to perform daily, small, unobtrusive acts of self-denial, such as omitting a tempting dessert as an act of love for God. The reason for this practice is that a habit of impurity is essentially a form of uncontrolled gratification.

All the suggestions I have made so far have been incorporated into a program for chastity for persons with homosexual tendencies. It is my opinion that heterosexual persons with sexual bad habits or addictions can profit by a similar program. Indeed, there is such a program that helps not only heterosexual persons, but also persons with same-sex attraction. It is Sexaholics Anonymous (SA), a twelve-step program similar to Alcoholics Anonymous (AA). The steps in the two programs are identical, with one exception—in S.A., step one speaks of personal powerlessness over sexual addiction (in place of alcohol, as in AA).[3]

5. How can I protect—and grow in—the virtue of chastity?

Traditionally, modesty in matters of sexuality has been seen as a natural protection of the virtue of chastity. St. Thomas Aquinas regarded modesty as part of the virtue of chastity.[4] Although chastity is a gift of God, it is expected of the person receiving the gift to use the means of protecting it, namely, modesty. One needs to discipline the external senses of sight, hearing, touch, and smell, as well as the internal powers of memory and imagination. In brief, the grace of chastity demands of us the practice of modesty, which, in turn, involves both self-discipline and honest acceptance of our limitations.

A few examples are in order. A person with same-sex attraction must avoid gay bars, magazines, and Internet websites, just as a heterosexual person should not go to movies and night clubs which hold chastity in contempt. Continued association with another person with same-sex attraction when one is aware that there is a *probability* that one may fall into sin is both dishonest and immodest. The same principle applies to a heterosexual unmarried couple who has already violated chastity and get into the same situation in which they had previously fallen.

6. **What kind of support is there to help me practice chastity?**

As you read through the following chapters, you will discern that the main issue at hand is the need for chastity, which is a gift from God, and at the same time, an obligation. We are obligated to practice it, but we cannot without God's grace.

As you read through chapter 4, you may have realized that the main battle is over the issue of marriage. Marriage is the objective norm for the practice of chastity; it makes room for the lawful exercise of sexuality. In that chapter, it is stated that gay "marriage" is a complete violation of the norm of marriage. It does away with all norms for the exercise of sexuality.

Having stated these truths, we need to go on to work out programs for the practice of chastity. For example, Courage came into existence as a program to help persons with same-sex attraction remain chaste. People who come to Courage meetings know that they need the support of the group to strengthen their resolve to remain chaste. Another example is a group called Sexaholics Anonymous, which we have already mentioned. It is interdenominational, but most of the persons who go are Christians. These people benefit by constantly attending meetings where they meet others with the same kinds of difficulties they have. This leads to a sense of solidarity with the other members. For example, at some Catholic college campuses, young people join together to help each other practice chastity. They share common ideals, entering into a spirit of prayer.

One development within Courage, beginning in 1990, was the formation of the first Courage Reparational Prayer Group. Writing about the group, journalist Susan Brinkmann notes that one of the main reasons it was formed was because "chastity is hard for anybody in our sex-saturated culture."[5] Vera, the founder, says: "We come together to offer up our struggle with chastity and use it as a reparation for the sins of the world. We offer up our own pain and struggle, and unite it with the passion of Jesus to bring life to others. It gives meaning to our suffering."[6] The Philadelphia group meets once a month for a talk on the interior life, personal sharing, and a holy hour, during which they pray especially "for those who are struggling with homosexual feelings." Groups have also been formed in several other states.[7]

7. Is there anyone who has really gone beyond "white-knuckled" chastity and lived it joyfully?

Yes. St. Augustine describes the conflicted state of mind that was the result of his many years of indulgence in lust. As he approached the Catholic faith, he still found that he was not able to be chaste. In his own words, "The new will which I now began to have to serve thee for thyself and to enjoy thee, O God...was not yet able to master that other, which had been established by so long an habituation."[8]

Actually, St. Augustine did not remain long in this conflicted state. In book 8, chapter 12 of his *Confessions*, he describes his conversion in the garden. He notes that he was in torturous indecision until he read Romans 13:13-14: "Let us conduct ourselves becomingly as in the day, not in debauchery and licentiousness, not in quarreling and jealousy. But put on the Lord Jesus Christ, and make no provision for the flesh, to gratify its desires."

Augustine then recalls: "I had no wish to read further, and no need. For in that instant, with the very ending of the sentence, it was as though a light of utter confidence shone in all my heart, and all the darkness of uncertainty vanished away."[9]

Book 9, chapter 1 of *Confessions* testifies to the profound change that had taken place within his heart at the time of his conversion to Christ. Previously, he was afraid that he could not do without lustful pleasures; now he says: "How lovely I suddenly found it to be free from the loveliness of those vanities so that now it was a joy to renounce what I had been so afraid to lose. For you cast them out of me and took their place in me; You who are sweeter than all pleasure, yet not to flesh and blood."[10]

Augustine's conversion was extraordinary in that he did not have the struggles that many converts experience in the practice of chastity. He immediately received the gift of interior chastity, as his words indicate. He is a source of joy to all those who struggle against lust. With his conversion he entered into a deep life of prayer, and that prayer of the heart led to chastity of the heart.

In Courage, we teach that one can move from a struggling continence to chastity of the heart. We stress fidelity to meditation, the formation of chaste friendships, honesty with oneself, and avoidance of near occasions of sin. While we are concerned that our members seek to reduce same-sex attractions and happy to see some get rid of them, we focus our energies on the development of a spiritual life, while keeping in contact with Catholic therapists.

8. What Scripture passages specifically relate to chastity?

St. Paul seeks to awaken in us a sense of awe and respect for the great dignity God has bestowed on our bodies when he says:

> The body is not meant for immorality, but for the Lord, and the Lord for the body...Do you not know that your bodies are members of Christ? Shall I therefore take the members of Christ and make them members of a prostitute? Never! Do you not know that he who joins himself to a prostitute becomes one body with her? For as it is written, 'The two shall become one.' But he who is united to the Lord becomes one spirit with him. Shun immorality. Every other sin a man commits is outside the body; but the immoral man sins against his own body. Do you not know that your body is a temple of the Holy Spirit within you, which you have from God? You are not your own; you were bought with a price. So glorify God in your body (1 Cor 6:13-20).[11]

The following three texts refer to immodesty as forms of unchastity:

* In the Sermon on the Mount, Jesus says, "But I say to you that every one who looks at a woman lustfully has already committed adultery with her in his heart" (Mt 5:28).

- "Immorality and all impurity or covetousness must not even be named among you...Let there be no filthiness, nor silly talk, nor levity, which are not fitting; but instead let there be thanksgiving" (Eph 5:3-4).

- "They have eyes full of adultery, insatiable for sin. They entice unsteady souls. They have hearts trained in greed" (2 Pt 2:14).

These words of Holy Scripture should be pondered as a personal basis for the practice of interior chastity. However, the *gift* of chastity will only come through prayer.

9. **Is chastity, then, the virtue that helps us to save sex for marriage?**

Yes. Paragraph 2337 of the *Catechism* mentions chastity within marriage as well. Marital chastity is concerned with the integration of the bodily and spiritual being in the relationship of husband and wife. This "integral vision of man" (a phrase used by Pope Paul VI in his encyclical *Humanae Vitae*) was elaborated on by Pope John Paul II in a series of Wednesday catechetical discourses that he gave over several years. In these 129 weekly addresses, John Paul II presents his profound Theology of the Body.[12]

Of course, since everyone is called to live chastely, this virtue assumes other forms as well: that of the adolescent; that of the unmarried adult, including widows and widowers; that of those who have taken private vows of chastity; that of the diocesan priest; and that of the consecrated religious (i.e., consecrated celibacy). The lay single state includes the unmarried, widows, and widowers.

Not to be overlooked is the special chastity lived by Joseph and Mary as husband and wife.

10.   What is the Theology of the Body?

Referencing the first two chapters of Genesis, Pope John Paul II taught that the human body is integral to the human person. In Genesis 1:27, we can see the differentiation of the sexes as part of the divine plan: "So God created man in his own image, in the image of God he created him; male and female he created them." In the next verse, the purpose of the differentiation of the sexes is found in the divine blessing: "Be fruitful and multiply" (Gn 1:28). As Joseph Martino puts it, "We do not possess our bodies as if they were apart from us; rather we are body persons. God created us bodily persons and communal in nature by being related to him and one another."[13]

Turning to Genesis 2:18, we read, "It is not good that the man should be alone; I will make him a helper fit for him." God indeed made a suitable partner for Adam: "Therefore a man leaves his father and his mother and cleaves to his wife and they become one flesh" (Gn 2:24).

This is the complementarity of the sexes, for a married couple truly is one body—the husband receiving the wife and the wife receiving the husband. Sexual relations within marriage also unite the spouses spiritually; their act of love is not only a communion of their bodies, but also a union of their wills. The Creator intended that sexual intercourse should be an act of love between husband and wife in which their communion of bodies may lead to the procreation of a child. In this act of marital intercourse the husband gives his whole person to the wife and the wife gives her whole person to the husband. They are not mere instruments of procreation; they are two subjects in a common unity. All this is the teaching of John Paul II, which emphasizes the "nuptial meaning of the body."[14]

11. Does contraception fit in with such a view of marriage?

No. In contraceptive intercourse, there is no true union of bodies. Contraception destroys the meaning of the marital act by nullifying the procreative power of the act of intercourse. Pope Paul VI stated the teaching of the Church in *Humanae Vitae*: "There is an unbreakable connection between the unitive and procreative meaning, and both are inherent in the conjugal act. God established this connection and man is not permitted to break it through his own volition."[15]

The marital act, then, has two inseparable purposes, one unitive and one procreative. Through their bodily and spiritual union in sexual relations, spouses strengthen the communion of persons which is marriage. In addition, they are open to the possibility that their union will lead to the procreation of a child.

Interestingly, even the father of psychoanalysis (and an avowed agnostic), Sigmund Freud, was in basic agreement with *Humanae Vitae* when he said, "The abandonment of the reproductive function is the common feature of all perversions. We actually describe a sexual activity as perverse if it has given up the aim of reproduction and pursues the attainment of pleasure as an aim independent of it."[16]

12. But hasn't *Humanae Vitae* been ignored—and even contradicted—by many within the Church?

Tragically for the Church throughout the world, *Humanae Vitae* was rejected by many Catholic leaders, clergy and laity alike, when it was promulgated in 1968. This rejection opened the door for more permissive attitudes among Catholics toward sex outside of marriage, abortion, cohabitation, divorce, pornography, the homosexual lifestyle, and, most recently, same-sex "marriage." In an article in *Catholic World Report,* Bishop Joseph Martino quotes Flannery O'Connor, calling the Church's doctrine on contraception "the most absolutely spiritual of all her stands." Then, O'Connor added a catch: "With all of us being materialists at heart, there is little wonder that it causes us unease."[17]

As a moral theologian for more than fifty years, I have witnessed firsthand the moral devastation wrought on our Catholic laity by the lack of leadership among our bishops (with a few happy exceptions) and their failure to warn Catholics about the evil of contraception. Many priests, likewise, have either been silent on the issue or advised the laity to "follow their own conscience."

Today, nearly forty years after the issuance of *Humanae Vitae*, things are *beginning* to change. Thanks to some courageous leaders who have been lecturing and writing on chastity in all its forms, many of our high school and college students—as well as many adults—have been taught Natural Family Planning (NFP), as well as the meaning of consecrated celibacy.[18]

13. **According to recent surveys, though, the majority of married Catholics are still using contraceptives.**

Unfortunately, this does seem to be the case. There are still many Catholic married couples who regard contraceptive use as necessary to space their children. They do not view this practice as sinful or make it a matter of confession, probably because in their parish they seldom hear the evils of contraception explained from the pulpit. Meanwhile, the secular culture continues to propose contraceptives in sexual activity as being "responsible" and "safe."

Writing in *The Wanderer*, Paul Likoudis cites a study by the National Center for Health Statistics which states that contraceptive use "is virtually universal among women of reproductive age" and that ninety-eight percent of American women are using "at least" one contraceptive method while engaging in intercourse.[19] While these statistics may be somewhat inflated, they indicate that many Catholic women continue to practice contraception.

In view of the high percentage of American women practicing contraception with their partners, in or outside of marriage, it is no wonder that persons with same-sex attraction view contraceptive intercourse "because of love" as justification for homosexual activity "because of love." This also explains why so many heterosexual persons see nothing immoral in homosexual unions.

14. **Why don't we hear about this gift of chastity very often from the pulpit?**

There may be several reasons for this sad fact. A recent conversation I had with several priests left me with the impression that they did not believe that the virtue of chastity—especially as it relates to contraception—could be fully practiced by married couples. I was asked what kind of advice I would give to a couple who already have five children and do not believe that they can afford another child. Should I not recommend some form of contraception? After all, they have made their contribution to the human race, and isn't it asking too much that they refrain from intercourse because they cannot afford another child? I replied that there were other resources available to such couples, such as updated forms of Natural Family Planning (NFP), of which many Catholics are not aware.

The argument went on and on. Was I not being unreasonable regarding contraception as being sinful in such circumstances? I argued that sometimes a married person should give up intercourse with one's spouse for a good reason. Indeed, if there is true love between husband and wife, there will be many times when they must abstain from intercourse because of sickness, travel, or some other serious reason. On these occasions, their restraint from intercourse or from any form of solitary sex is really an act of love for the other person. In this age, when some married people think that if they have to refrain from intercourse for a time their love will be weakened, it is remarkable that others who willingly give up intercourse with their spouse temporarily for good reasons continue to have a loving relationship. Indeed, their mutual love becomes much stronger, as thousands of persons who have practiced NFP will attest.

15. But how many married couples can really live that kind of life?

Some years ago I knew a doctor who had been in a previous valid marriage, but was divorced by his wife because she was not satisfied with the income that he was able to provide. In the military during the Second World War, he married a Catholic woman in a civil ceremony and had two lovely little girls within a few years. He and his wife, however, began to feel guilty and longed to go to Holy Communion, but they could not since they were in an invalid marriage. Then he proposed to me that they would be willing to live together as brother and sister so that they could rear their children and be reconciled with the Church, and that is what they did.

Years later, I met one of the daughters in New York. She is a clinical psychologist, but she was not happy about living in the midst of prostitution and homosexuality in Manhattan. I said, "Living alone in Greenwich Village must be very difficult for you." She responded, "Father, my sister and I knew what my father and mother gave up in order to remain with us and lead us to adulthood. I know that was a real sacrifice of love, and it has always helped me in moments of temptation. I knew that they really loved each other and loved us as they remained celibate."

I wish the priests I spoke with could have had the experiences that I had with this couple who believed in—and lived—the truth of chastity. There is a need to reflect upon the virtue of chastity, especially as it relates to contraception, conjugal love, and persons with same-sex attraction.

NOTES

1   See Thomas Aquinas, *Summa Theologiae* I-II, 64, 1, and II-II, 151, 1. Another way of saying this is that one who has the virtue of chastity must, by definition, have feelings that are habitually moved in concert with reason (from chapter 1).

2   *Summa* II-II, 151, 1.

3   For more information, write to Sexaholics Anonymous, P.O. Box 300, Simi Valley, CA 93062 or visit their website, www.sa.org.

4   Aquinas, *Summa Theologiae*, II-II, 1, 51, 4. See "Modesty," by S. O'Riordan in *New Catholic Encyclopedia*, vol. 9, pp. 996-97.

5   Susan Brinkmann, "The Theology of Weakness: Courage Reparational Prayer Group," *Catholic Standard & Times* (Philadelphia), September 9, 2004.

6   Ibid.

7   For more information about the Courage Reparational Group, see the Courage website, www.couragerc.net, and follow the "Reparational Groups" link.

8   Augustine, *Confessions*, bk. 8, ch. 5, 10. See John Harvey, *The Moral Theology of the Confessions of St. Augustine*, pp. 83-85, 107-108.

9   Ibid., bk. 8, ch. 12; Frank Sheed trans. (London: Sheed and Ward, 1949), p.142.

10   Ibid., bk. 8, ch. 1.

11   See Christopher West, *Theology of the Body Explained* (Boston: Pauline, 2003), p. 219. Here, West is speaking of having a right mode of being pure: "Therefore, for St. Paul, purity and modesty must be centered on the dignity of the body—on the dignity of the person who is always expressed through the body, through his masculinity and her femininity."

12   See John Paul II, *The Theology of the Body: Human Love in the Divine Plan* (Boston: Pauline, 1997).

13   Joseph F. Martino, "Practicing Chastity in an Unchaste World," *Catholic World Report,* January 2005.

14   William E. May, "On the Impossibility of Same-Sex Marriage," *National Catholic Bioethics Quarterly* 4, no. 2 (Summer 2004): pp. 310-13.

15   *Humanae Vitae,* no. 12.

16   Sigmund Freud, *Introductory Lectures in Psychoanalysis* (New York: W.W. Norton, 1966), p. 392, quoted in Christopher West, *Theology of the Body Explained* (Boston: Pauline, 2003), p. 47.

17   Martino, pp. 56-60.

18   Among these leaders are Mary Beth Bonacci, author of *Real Love: Answers to Your Questions on Dating, Marriage, and the Real Meaning of Sex* (San Francisco: Ignatius, 1996) and *We Are on a Mission from God* (San Francisco: Ignatius, 1996), as well as numerous audio and video presentations; and Janet Smith, Ph.D., author of *Humanae Vitae: A Generation Later* (Washington, DC: Catholic University of America Press, 1991) and *Why Humanae Vitae? A Generation Later* (San Francisco: Ignatius, 1993). See also John Kippley, *Sex and Marriage Covenant: A Basis for Morality* (Couple to Couple League International, 1991).

19   "Government Study Says Contraceptive Use Nearly Universal," *The Wanderer* (January 13, 2005), p. 1.

CHAPTER 6

Human Friendships: Benefits and Boundaries

1. How do spiritual writers, including St. Francis de Sales, describe good friendships?

Spiritual writers apply the notion of friendship to our relationship with God. At the Last Supper, Jesus tells the apostles that He no longer calls them servants but friends (see Jn 15:15). He speaks of His oneness with His Heavenly Father and of our oneness with Him. In addition, Jesus promises to send the Holy Spirit to strengthen us. As a Trinity, the Father, Son, and Holy Spirit are all one in an everlasting friendship.

Reflecting on the true nature of friendship in his classic *Introduction to the Devout Life*, St. Francis de Sales writes, "The higher the virtues you share and exchange with others, the more perfect your friendship will be. If your mutual and reciprocal exchanges concern charity and Christian perfection...how precious this friendship will be. It will be excellent because it comes from God, excellent because it leads to God, excellent because its bond will endure eternally in God."[1]

St. Francis de Sales' understanding of the various forms of friendship is discussed throughout six chapters of the *Introduction to the Devout Life*.[2] St. Francis first distinguishes between love and friendship. It may happen, for example, that one person loves another, but the latter does not reciprocate the affection. In friendship, love is mutual; furthermore, both persons recognize their mutual love, and they seek to share ideas and affection as they communicate regularly with each other.

In addition, St. Francis holds that friendship "is the most dangerous of all types of love, since other kinds may be had without intercommunication, but friendship is completely based on it, and we can hardly have such communication with a person without sharing in the other person's qualities."[3]

2.   Are there different kinds of friendships?

Yes. Friendships differ according to the kind of goods which are exchanged. If the goods are false and empty, the friendship is false and empty. If the goods exchanged are true goods, the friendship is true—and the better the goods are, the better the friendship.[4] Marriage is an example of an exchange of true goods. In marriage, "there is an exchange of life, work, goods, affection and indissoluble fidelity. Marriage is, therefore, a true holy friendship."[5]

In sharp contrast, sexual relations outside of the bond of marriage are immoral and dehumanizing. As St. Francis puts it, "Exchange of carnal pleasures involves mutual inclinations and animal allurement. It has no more right to the title of friendship among men than that of asses and horses for like effects."[6]

With regard to evil friendships, or even friendships which could be regarded as dangerous to both parties because of their mutual immaturity and vulnerability, the usually gentle St. Francis declares, "Cut them. Break them. Rip them apart...You must tear and rip them apart...Do not enter into any compromise with a love so opposed to the love of God."[7] He adds that we must not deceive ourselves into believing that we can handle such a situation.

3. How should we choose our friends?

St. Francis de Sales repeats that one should form friendships only with those who can exchange virtues with you. The higher the virtues one can share with another, the more perfect the friendship will be. St. Francis calls this "spiritual friendship." By it, "two, three, or more souls share with one another their devotion and spiritual affections, and establish a single spirit among themselves … I hold that all other friendships are mere shadows in comparison with this, and that their bonds are but chains of glass … when compared with this bond of holy devotion, for it is made entirely of gold."[8] (Francis makes it clear that he is referring to the friendships which one chooses, not to the love of family.)

St. Francis goes on to say that friendships based upon the love of Christ are the best of all. Here, he is speaking of friendships which one chooses for oneself. He also wants us to cherish the friendships among family members and relatives. St. Francis does not stop there. Referring to Catholic laypeople, he says that it is necessary to unite together in holy sacred friendship. In this way, they encourage one another to live lives in union with Christ. St. Francis recalls that Jesus Himself had special friends in John the Apostle, Mary Magdalene, Martha , Mary, and Lazarus. Among the saints, one finds many examples of deep friendships, such as Basil the Great and Gregory Nazianzen, Francis of Assisi and Clare, and Francis de Sales and Jane de Chantal. For those seeking God, holy friendships are a great benefit.[9] It will be necessary later, however, to discuss the boundaries of friendship.

4.   Didn't St. Augustine also teach on friendship?

Yes. Jesus, in His human and divine natures, seeks friendship with each person. St. Augustine enlarges upon the notion of God as the bond of human friendship when he says, "Blessed is the man who loves thee, and his friend in thee, and his enemy for thee. For he alone never loses a dear friend, to whom all men are dear for his sake who is never lost. And who is this but our God."[10]

According to Augustine, the solution of the problem of human friendship lies in the integration of the love of man with the love of God. One loves the friend as the image of God; one loves his enemy because God has commanded it, and because the sinful soul still retains the divine image, however blurred, as well as the capacity for divine grace.

It must not be forgotten that the goodness one loves in his friend comes from God and must be referred back to Him. Persons must be loved in God. One presents, as it were, his friend to God. Filled with love, one exhorts his friend to love God, realizing that whatever is beautiful in his friendship is a divine gift. On the other hand, he who abandons God in his quest for human love will suffer the bitterness of a false friendship. God must be in human friendships, or they will contain no true happiness.[11]

In developing the gift of charity infused into our hearts by the Holy Spirit, the individual is able to love the divine goodness as it is reflected in His creatures. In this way the virtue of charity prepares us for human friendships. Again, as St. Augustine learned by bitter experience, God must be in human friendships, or they will contain no true happiness.

This general principle leads to two perennially practical conclusions: 1) a true friendship does not exist unless God be the bond between the friends; and 2) the solution of the problem of human friendship lies in the integration of the love of man with the love of God. Far from opposing human friendship to the divine, one realizes that whatever is beautiful in his friendship is a gift from God.[12]

In *The Four Loves*, C.S. Lewis makes an important distinction between purely affective, sentimental relationships and true friendships. A true friendship is a communion of ideals and affection in which two persons share with one another their common pursuit of a goal; for example, two people intent on defending the life of the unborn child. As they pursue their common goal, they come to realize that they are friends. Lewis adds that each thinks he knows when their friendship began; actually, it began before either realized it.[13]

5. **How should a person with same-sex attraction work on fostering good friendships?**

A person with SSA needs to place Jesus Christ first in his desires and affections. Much as he may desire intimacy and friendship with others, he realizes that he cannot express his affections and desires by acts which are contrary to his love for Christ and to the meaning of human sexuality, as described in the first two chapters of Genesis and in Matthew 19:3-8. He realizes that he must find ways of expressing affection chastely, that is to say, ways in which he has control of illicit and impure desires, while not tempting another person to impure acts. Chastity is found in the pure affections of the heart, and it is nourished by prayer. Thus, members of Courage seek friendships with other persons—including other Courage members—who share the teaching of the Church on sexual desires and behaviors.

The person with SSA will have a more difficult time in practicing chastity than will a heterosexual person, for a simple reason: a heterosexual can seek the special and exclusive friendship of marriage to fulfill his or her desire for sexual intimacy with another person of the opposite sex. But the man or woman with SSA does not have this option as long as he or she lacks the physical and genital attraction to persons of the other sex. He is bound to live a life rooted in chastity—something not possible by his purely human powers, but possible by the grace of God, as is proven by many with SSA who are leading chaste lives.

6. Can people with SSA develop friendships with other persons from both sexes while remaining chaste?

Yes. They can develop intimate, chaste friendships with other persons of both sexes. The second part of the video *Portraits of Courage*, entitled "The Cry of the Faithful," shows that persons with SSA can and do have close friends who share the common goal of chastity.[14] In this video, members of Courage can be seen together at meetings, games, prayer, and socials, demonstrating that the support of other Courage members is, along with God's grace, an important factor in living a chaste life.

While some people with SSA may be tempted to form an overly close relationship with one friend to the exclusion of others, they realize that they will pay too high a price for such an attempt at intimacy. As therapist Dr. William

Consiglio has pointed out, they are far better off to "hang out" with the group.

So one can form close friendships with several members of the group (or even outside the group) while practicing daily meditations with Jesus. But does this mean that one cannot prefer one friend over another? No, as long as he or she continues to remain in the group and to regard everyone in the group as worthy of his or her love. When a Courage member forms an exclusive friendship with another member, though, there is a danger of emotional overdependence and the sexualization of the relationship. Moral boundaries are usually violated.

7. **What kind of boundaries are necessary for someone with same-sex attraction to keep a close friendship from becoming sexualized?**

In counseling persons with SSA, I stress the value of expressing affection in a chaste way when in the company of other persons of the same sex with SSA. One observes the same boundaries as heterosexual men and women do by avoiding any conduct that will directly arouse feelings of lust within oneself or within the other person. Such conduct includes long telephone conversations, the exchanging of mutual affection, or using the Internet for the same purpose. Avoiding such behaviors can be described as putting in place an external boundary.

But there is also an internal boundary or protection found in the emotions and heart of the person. If the person practices prayer of the heart regularly, and places the love of Christ above that of any other person, he will have a sensitive conscience, generally avoiding near occasions of sin. Thus, in maintaining purity of heart, he has created an internal boundary within his conscience. In short, the interior life of prayer is the more important boundary.

If, however, one lacks an internal boundary in his conscience, he is more likely to violate the external boundaries, often rationalizing that he can handle an occasion of sin, and more often than not failing against purity. It is my experience as a spiritual director that an honest conscience, which recognizes one's own vulnerability to fantasy and lust, is the guardian of purity of heart.

There is another consideration which can help a person with SSA who tends to be overdependent upon another to the point where he makes the other person an idol. His whole emotional life is centered on that person. Though the other person may not feel a reciprocal dependence, he or she should withdraw from an intimate relationship with the overdependent individual.

In his *Confessions*, the young bishop Augustine describes his own past overdependence upon another young man whom he had converted to Manichaeism. The young man, however, came back to the Christian faith but died shortly afterward. Augustine plunged into a very profound depression. He was not yet converted. All seemed dark around him for quite a while, but he recovered and later received the grace of conversion. Describing the state of his soul, Augustine muses, "O madness that knows not how to love men as men."[15] Augustine was on target. No person, however holy, can satisfy the deep yearnings of the human heart; only God can do so. "Thou hast made us for Thyself, O Lord, and our hearts are ne'er at rest until they rest in Thee."[16] St. Francis de Sales adds that in every human friendship there is something lacking, because our hearts are made for union with Jesus Christ.

8.   **What role does friendship play in the lives of Courage members?**

One of the members of Courage wrote a piece called "The Three Pillars of Courage." The importance of friendship comes through in several places, and I would like to share it here:

The Three Pillars of Courage

I think of these as the three pillars of Courage—the support group setting, the rock-solid Catholic spirituality, the fellowship. In the group we remind ourselves of the Five Goals, especially our focus on developing lives of interior chastity (Goal One). At my Courage support group loving priests listen with compassion, and gently but firmly instruct us in the full truth of the Church's teachings. They bring medicine to our souls by giving us the truth with love and patience. In the Courage group I've also found moral support and encouragement from brothers and sisters in Christ who share my struggles and temptations. It's been a great comfort to me to be heard and understood by those who have "been there" and know what it's like to walk this walk. Sometimes falls may occur. But if we recognize a fall for what it is, we call sin by its name, go to confession, and move on. We take steps to avoid future occasions of sin, and keep ourselves accountable to our confessor/spiritual director.

The second pillar of Courage is the encouragement to deepen our Catholic spirituality and live it out. Those of us with same-sex attraction and a desire for chastity *know* that we need grace to achieve that goal, and where do we find that grace but in the spiritual riches of our Catholic Church—through the liturgy and reception of the Holy Eucharist, through confession, adoration, the Rosary, through private and group prayer, Scripture reading, meditation, and spiritual direction. We learn to come before God in absolute naked honesty about our emotional weaknesses and temptations, and our hunger for love—and there before the Blessed Sacrament, we receive love, peace, acceptance and healing.

The third pillar of Courage is fellowship. I'm fortunate to live in a part of the country where members get together regularly for fellowship, whether for sharing a meal, going on retreat together, going to the movies, or just getting together over a cup of coffee. We're also learning to involve ourselves in social and spiritual activities outside of Courage as part of the larger Church.

These three pillars—the support group, our Catholic spirituality, and good fellowship—all are aids to Courage members, no matter what our state in life, helping us live full lives of holiness and joy, in communion with one another and with the greater body of Christ.

9. **Could you sum up what you have said about chaste friendships, especially for persons with SSA?**

Using quotations from saints and scholars, I have reviewed the great benefits of chaste friendships. I have also pointed out the difference between external boundaries or limitations and the need for internal boundaries. Both are important, but the internal are more necessary because they come from the deepest part of the person— what biblical authors term the heart. The heart is really the total commitment of the will to a particular goal, for example, to be fully chaste in our thoughts and actions. This is possible only by the grace of God. In Augustine's words, chastity is a gift of God dependent upon prayer.

To keep chaste friendships one must fully admit one's own vulnerabilities and not pretend that one can handle the situation, which is usually a near occasion of sin. Humility—the loving admission of one's own limitations—helps preserve chastity.

The following observation is meant principally for persons with SSA. Recently a distinguished counselor from a Catholic university told me that persons with SSA make a mistake when they limit their close friendships to other persons with SSA. I have noticed this phenomenon among both women and men. The counselor recommended that men with SSA also form chaste friendships with heterosexual men, and that women with SSA do likewise with heterosexual women. This is good counsel.

Toward the end of the first Courage conference, held in Riverdale, New York, in 1989, Dr. Maria Valdes made the point that male persons with SSA should cultivate friendships with heterosexual men as well as with other persons with SSA. In the question-and-answer period following her presentation, Dr. Valdes received an objection from one of the men, who said, "I am afraid to form an intimate friendship with a heterosexual male person, because he might reject me as a gay person." She responded: "That's the problem...You assume all heterosexual persons will reject you. It's one, two, three strikes—you're out." This is a false assumption. Many persons with SSA have learned the value of close friendships with heterosexual persons, male and female. Those who do not do so restrict unnecessarily their choices to form chaste friendships, and often become too dependent upon another person with SSA.

Over the past twenty-four years, I have seen such overdependent persons and have tried to help them. Usually the overdependent person is the younger one, looking for a father; sometimes the other person does not know what to do. He tries to avoid the younger person, but without success, because the younger person pursues him. In this situation I persuaded the younger person to see a clinical psychologist. The older man kept his distance and wisely decided to break off the relationship.

Each of us needs to recognize that human friendships can help us find peace of heart in this world, provided we bring them to our personal relationship with Christ. The overly dependent person, above all, needs a relationship with Christ to counter fantasy quests for the perfect person.

The person seeking purity of heart will have no room for an attitude of casuistry, that is to say, "How far may I go before I go too far and give in to lust?" Another form of casuistry is to attribute one's failures to weakness of will. To this St. Augustine responds that it is not weakness of will, but a divided will, so to speak, which is the source of our difficulty. As a spiritual faculty, the will has its own unity and therefore cannot be divided. The will, however, is caught between an illicit desire *(lust)* and a good desire *(chastity)*. As long as it only partially wills chastity, it goes nowhere. As soon as it totally wills chastity—and totally rejects lust—it becomes unified, and can act for chastity. The grace to do so comes from the Holy Spirit. Thus there is only a unified will or a divided will.

In his treatment of friendship, St. Francis de Sales exhorts his readers to be rigorously honest with themselves, avoiding the myriad rationalizations of the evil one. I want to reiterate that the most important boundary is the determination of how one will practice chastity, which one ought to regard as a precious gift.

One may hope that through the practice of chastity and the cultivation of good friendships one may come to more fully embrace interior chastity, or chastity of the heart, through a deeper friendship with Christ.

Notes

1 Francis de Sales, *Introduction to the Devout Life*, trans. John K. Ryan (New York: Harper and Row, 1966; New York: Image, Doubleday, 1989), pt. 3, ch. 19.

2 Ibid., pt. 3, ch. 17-22.

3 Ibid., pt. 3, ch. 17.

4 Ibid.

5 Ibid.

6 Ibid., pt. 3, ch. 19.

7 Ibid., pt. 3, ch. 21.

8 Ibid., pt. 3, ch. 19.

9 Ibid.

10 *Confessions*, 4, 9, 14.

11 Harvey, *Moral Theology*, pp.36-38.

12 Ibid., p. 37.

13 C.S. Lewis, *The Four Loves* (New York: Harcourt Brace Jovanovich, 1960), pp. 81-83, 87-111.

14 This video can be ordered by calling 1-866-232-4278 or online at the Courage website, www.couragerc.net.

15 *Confessions*, 4, 7, 1.

16 Ibid., 1, 1, 1.

CHAPTER 7

Freedom of the Will and Addiction

On this important topic, we will take St. Augustine as our guide. His writings on the nature of the will and addiction are considered by moral theologians to be among the most profound among Christian thinkers.

1. **St. Augustine lived and wrote more than 1,500 years ago. Are his thoughts relevant for today?**

St. Augustine's experience of conversion and the struggles he went through to attain peace in his heart and mind are instructive for all, but especially for those who struggle with same-sex attraction. In order to understand the steps leading to his conversion, I think it will be helpful to examine first St. Augustine's pre-conversion experiences as a Manichean.

The Manicheans held that there were two eternal principles or causes of all things, the principle of light (which was good) and the principle of darkness (which was evil). These two principles, thought to be eternal, were engaged in unceasing strife with each other. Both principles were considered to be material, and hence all things were composed of matter. Thus, evil was considered a material substance.[1]

Since Augustine believed that there were two material principles in conflict with one another, he also believed that there were two material wills in conflict within each individual. This led him to believe that the evil principle was responsible for his evil acts. Gradually, as he moved away from such Manichean beliefs, he began to understand the spirituality of the human will and the spiritual nature of the good God.[2] But he still spoke of his "evil nature" overcoming his better nature. This was willful blindness. He was afraid to admit to himself that he desired the pleasures of lustful behavior.

Augustine did not yet understand that God is pure spirit—and that evil is not a substance, but the *privation* (i.e., lack) of a substance. Being a Manichaean, he regarded evil as a physical entity; he could not understand how an all-good God could create evil. Only when he came to understand that evil was not a substance but merely a privation was he able to see clearly that the will of man was the cause of sin, and that God merely tolerates evil.

As he overcame his false beliefs, Augustine formulated an argument that man's will is the cause of sin. God is incorruptible, inviolable, and immutable, but every creature is corruptible, violable, and mutable. Therefore, man as a creature can sin, and through habitual sin, subject himself to forces over which he has little or no control, such as an addiction.

In his *Confessions*, St. Augustine writes about how he came to realize this truth. During his Manichean darkness, he was accustomed to blaming the foreign substance within him for his sins, but as he drew closer to the truth, he saw that he alone was responsible for his deliberate actions. Finally, during a crisis he experienced just before his conversion, Augustine perceived that the Manichean doctrine of two wills, one good and one bad, fighting for supremacy within man, was unreasonable. He realized that it was not a question of conflicting wills, but rather of conflicting desires within a man's soul. For there is but one soul—a soul with one will—in a human being. This will, however, can be attracted by many different objects and be tormented by many conflicting desires. Assigning a separate will to every desire would mean a ridiculous multiplication of wills in the individual.

2. **How did Augustine's new understanding help him grow in virtue?**

Even after Augustine's mind grasped the truth, a gap between his knowledge about virtue and his ability to practice it remained. On the brink of his conversion, for example, he desired not greater certitude concerning God but more stability in pursuing Him. Augustine knew what he ought to do, but he hesitated for fear that following Christ might prove too arduous for one who had been accustomed to gratifying his sensual appetites. His mind had received light, yet his affections needed purification.

> But as touching my temporal life, all things were still unresolved, and my heart was yet to be delivered more fully from the old leaven. The Way, the Savior of the World, did please me well, but I could not find it in my heart to follow it through the strait gate.[3]

Even though he was displeased with himself, he continued to live in carnal pleasure, considering himself too weak to embrace the higher life of chastity. He was convinced that it would be much better for him to dedicate himself to God than to indulge his own cupidity. Thus, pleasure kept him enslaved, and he could not form the resolution to do what he should do. What was lacking was not strength of will but purpose and motivation.[4]

3. What conflicts did Augustine have to fight to break his enslavement to sin?

Augustine had two conflicts to fight: the conflict between the flesh and the spirit, and the conflict between spirit and spirit—and he believed the latter conflict to be just as fierce as the first. This latter conflict is linked with the failure to integrate one's actions under one dominant purpose or aim.

With regard to the first conflict (spirit against flesh), Augustine follows St. Paul, who says in Romans 6:1-14 that the law of God according to the inner man is in conflict with that other law in his members, drawing him down to sins of the flesh. Following St. Paul, Augustine teaches that only the grace of Christ can overcome the rebellious tendencies of the flesh.[5]

Augustine discusses the battle between flesh and spirit in terms of habit. As I have previously mentioned, at the beginning of his battle against the flesh, before he understood the will to be one but divided, he wrote: "But the new will was not able as yet to master that other which had been established by so long continuance. Thus did my two wills, one old and the other new, one carnal and the other spiritual, fight one against the other and by their discord did they drag my soul asunder."[6]

With regard to the battle of spirit against spirit, the struggle is different. After the conversion of his friend Pontitianus, Augustine had entered profoundly into himself and remonstrated with himself for his delay in embracing the Christian life. At that time, he did not know the root of his procrastination. But later, writing in the *Confessions*, he put his finger on the sore spot and diagnosed it as a divided will which was therefore maimed, leaving him in a state of indecision and inaction.[7] The battle between spirit and spirit is a battle of the will with itself.

4.   **Could you explain more about having a "divided will"?**

St. Augustine explains that willing and doing are so intimately linked that when one wills something *resolutely*, it is the beginning of *doing*. They are but two different aspects of one and the same human act. But this is precisely where the difficulty lies. The body more easily obeys the weakest nod of the soul, moving one of its limbs, than the will carries out its own command.

> Why is this so? Why does the will have immediate power over bodily members, and not over its bodily self? Again, the answer is the same...What the mind commands itself to do is not done, because it does not command it entirely (*totaliter*). At the same time, *part of its energy* is being absorbed by some other object, and this prevents the *execution of the plan*.[8]

When the will is unified, then to will the command is the same thing as to command. "The fact of indecision, partly to will something, and partly not to will it, is a disease of the mind."[9] The will is drawn in contrary directions at one and the same time. While the goal of truth pulls it upwards, the goal of inveterate carnal pleasure drags it downwards; the consequence is indecision. More accurately, it may be said that one is attracted by contrary objects but does not will either one. In other words, two partial wills are equivalent to no will. No matter how much an individual deliberates, he remains in a moral rut as long as he forms no resolute purpose of amendment.

Augustine points to his delay as an example of the effects of a divided will in the practical moral life. Since he did not will his conversion entirely, he delayed it and remained in sin.

5. **So is there any difference between a divided will and a will that is merely weak?**

On this point, St. Augustine's analysis exposes another common misconception. He shows that weakness of will is really an illusion. The will is not weak or strong; rather, it is divided or unified. It is divided when it is drawn in contrary directions by contrary motives; it is unified when it concentrates on its goal with singleness of purpose.

Again, Augustine refers to the problem of a divided will when he writes,

> The trouble [with a divided will] is that it does not totally will, therefore it does not totally command. It commands insofar as it wills and it disobeys the command in so far as it does not will. The will is commanding itself to be a will—commanding itself, not some other. But it does not in its fullness give the command, so that what it commands is not done. For if the will were so in its fullness, it would not command itself to will, for it would already will.[10]

In his commentary on this passage, Rudolf Allers notes that real willing and doing are but two sides of one and the same human act. He points out that "weakness of will is in truth an illusion or self-deception of the mind, resulting from a man's striving for two—or even more—goals at the same time; what is called weakness of will is not due so much to lack of energy as to lack of unity of the will. The trouble lies more with purpose than with will."[11]

To will something directly and fully is the Saint's expression for a resolution of a divided will. In attempting to change a divided will to a unified will, a person can rely on God, who gives grace. With the gift of supernatural grace, the person becomes able to will *entirely* (*totaliter*). After his conversion, Augustine's will was, shall we say, magnetized by the Divine Beauty, so much so that he could exclaim that God was sweeter than all earthly pleasure. God compensated him beyond measure for the renunciation of all carnal pleasures, pleasures he thought he couldn't do without.

It is clear that cooperation with grace will bring singleness of aim or unity of will into the life of a person afflicted with the same sort of indecision as Augustine. God can cause man to be ravished by Divine Beauty and to be filled with the desire of union with God. Whenever this happens, the will is no longer forcibly drawn by conflicting values of earth.

6. **How can Augustine's analysis of the will help me in my daily life?**

Since moral acts—i.e., human acts—are essentially acts of the will, one may draw from Augustine's penetrating analysis of the will in the *Confessions* some conclusions for living well. So far, we have noted that the *Confessions* discusses not only the conflict between the flesh and the spirit, but also the battle between the spirit and the spirit. In this latter conflict, the will attempts to follow several conflicting goals simultaneously, and this leads inevitably to indecision and so-called "weakness" of will. The remedy is to concentrate the will on one goal to the exclusion of all incompatible aims. In other words, the solution to the problem of a divided will is a singleness of purpose that integrates all the faculties of the soul—the whole person— in doing the will of God in all things.

The very formation and accomplishment of such a resolution is itself a gift of divine grace, as Augustine attests:

> But Thou, O Lord, are gracious and merciful, and thy right hand had regard to the profundity of my death, and from the bottom of my heart it drew forth that huge bulk of corruption. And this deliverance, what was it, but that I willed not any more that which I was wont to will, but I willed what you willed.¹²

The will finds strength to pursue the object of its happiness as soon as it cooperates with divine grace and forms the wholehearted and effective resolution to put the goal of its happiness—God—first in its scale of values.

7.   How do Augustine's insights help someone with addictions?

Actually, they have great value for persons with addictions, whether to alcohol, drugs, masturbation, or pornography— and for spiritual counselors of those with addictions. We have previously suggested the need for the individual to develop a personal plan of life, not only to overcome a sinful habit but also to draw closer to Christ in prayer.

On the human level, though, the implementation of such a plan depends upon wholehearted cooperation with the grace of God. The person with an addiction must ask himself: Do I *really* will to avoid masturbation, pornography, or any other bad habit? If so, am I willing to take the series of steps proposed by counselors? Am I willing to make it a matter of reflection and prayer? In making these proposals I am *not* saying that one must depend upon pure willpower or purely human motivation. One needs the guidance of the Holy Spirit, together with faith, hope, and charity, and the four moral virtues of prudence, fortitude, justice, and temperance (of which chastity is a part). Some individuals may also need counseling and spiritual direction.

8. **What other insights about the will does Augustine have for counselors and spiritual directors?**

There are several other aspects of the will discussed in the *Confessions* that provide insight. The first is the connection between the rebellion within man and original sin. In his investigation into the cause of sin before his conversion, Augustine had observed that certain motions took place in him but *against* his will. These he regarded not as sins but as punishment for sin. He writes, "Whatsoever I did unwillingly [*invitus*], I saw that I did suffer rather than do, and I esteemed that not to be a fault but a punishment." Here the Latin term *invitus,* which is translated "unwillingly," may refer to the involuntary motions of concupiscence (i.e., strong desires for inordinate pleasures), whose rebellion against reason is part of the punishment of original sin. To experience such motions without consenting to them is a punishment for original sin rather than an actual sin.

Augustine implies that division within the will is the common penalty of the sin of Adam. In the description of his infancy, he quotes Psalm 51:5 to the effect that he was born in sin, and then describes the "perversity" of infant behavior. He does not say that infants are responsible for their behaviors, but he does stress the truth that such tendencies can form the beginnings of bad habits.[13]

Another important aspect of will which Augustine discusses is habit, in the sense of a sinful pattern of behavior. In a classic passage, St. Augustine describes his enslavement to the habit of impurity, comparing the formation of the habit to a chain, which, forged, link by link, finally enslaves the will of its maker:

> For I aspired to do good, but I was bound as yet, albeit not with a chain of iron, but only with the chain of my untoward will. My enemy made fast this will of mine, and from it he forged the chain which bound me. For through the perverseness of our affection grows lust, and by yielding often to that lust we make a custom, and by not opposing this custom we grow subject to a kind of necessity. By these links fastened one within another—for which reason I have called it a chain—the bitter servitude held me bound.[14]

9. What are the stages a person goes through in forging this chain of enslavement to sin?

There are four key links in this moral chain: 1) *perverse will*. This is found in the first deliberate act of impurity, which is primarily a rebellion of the spirit against the law of God. It is the basic deorientation of the will from its highest good (God), which gives rise to the consequent rebellion of the flesh against the spirit, and such disobedience to God's law opens the way for the next stage, namely, 2) *libido* or *perverted lust*. The initial pleasure of lust stimulates and excites the individual to seek the same pleasure again, and with repetition comes the third stage, 3) *consuetudo* or *habit*, by which the soul is drawn powerfully to the vice it has sought frequently. Thus, an evil habit is formed from continued license; and, as this habit becomes more deeply entrenched, the fourth stage begins, and this may be termed 4) *necessity*. Just as a chain is gradually fashioned from the individual links, so the will is increasingly entangled by repeated acts of impurity until the individual believes that he *must* have the pleasure that comes from the operation of the habit. Consequently, he despairs of his ability to resist its violence and yields to its impulses, as if unavoidable.

In the first link, the person is conscious that he is sinning and feels guilty. But with the repetition of the sin, link two, conscience is worn down, and one gradually forms a bad habit. That habit may lead to necessity or addiction.

10. How do we apply Augustine's teaching to problems like masturbation and pornography?

First of all, what Augustine calls *necessity*, we would call *addiction*. In moral theology, habit is a pattern of acts. Some habits can be changed without resorting to professional counseling. For example, an individual might have a bad habit of drinking excessively during the Christmas holidays. With ordinary self-discipline he can learn to drink moderately in all seasons.

Another individual, though, might spend thousands of dollars on pornography. He lives alone, staying up all night watching pornographic films. He is an addict. He has a pseudo-relationship with a mind-altering experience, as described in chapter 3. He needs professional help and group support in organizations like Sexaholics Anonymous, and Sex and Love Addicts Anonymous. He also needs spiritual support systems like Courage.

11. Does a sex addict bear any responsibility for his actions if he truly cannot control them?

If a person deliberately performed impure acts and made no attempt to desist from them at the start, he is responsible to some extent for his subsequent addictive behavior. On the other hand, if he had no real awareness of the consequences of his actions, he may not be fully responsible for his subsequent actions. At the first two links in Augustine's chain, *perverse will* and *libido or perverted lust*, a person could have brought himself back to the practice of chastity. By the third link *(consuetudo or habit)*, though, little freedom remains, and when the person moves on to the fourth link, *necessity*, freedom is lost. The will that had abused its freedom in licentiousness becomes the slave of the very vice it had sought out; likewise, the guilt of habitual sins lies in one's culpability in forming the habit in the first place.

It should be noted that Augustine considered himself guilty of forming at least a bad habit of impurity which bordered on addiction. Actually, for several years, Augustine broke the chain of his bad habit, but grace enabled him to make the final break.

12. Is the *Confessions* useful in counseling and spiritual direction?

In both pastoral counseling and spiritual direction, I have used the texts of the *Confessions* to guide persons with serious sexual problems, particularly masturbation and pornography. Oftentimes individuals struggling with these problems are very discouraged with their failure to overcome these acts, and are happy to know that St. Augustine also had to battle similar temptations as a young adult. They identify with his rationalizations and procrastination. They learn how to draw up a plan of life. When they find themselves in a state of indecision, they ask themselves what do I really *want* to do and *will* to do. They see the need to focus continually on the spiritual goals of union with Jesus Christ and service to His Church. Personally, from my reflections on the *Confessions* I have gained insights not only for myself, but for those I have counseled over the years.

We can see Augustine's "chain" reflected in some contemporary psychological studies of addiction and bad habits, such as the books *Contrary to Love,* by Patrick Carnes, and *Addiction and Grace,* by Gerald G. May.[15] But there is also a striking difference between Augustine and Carnes, in that Augustine integrates the influence of divine grace with our free will.

The study of the factors which lead to the development of a unified will have ramifications in our spiritual life. It will make us more honest with ourselves, making us less prone to rationalize our sins and failures. It will encourage us in our work for the Lord, knowing that when we will a good action with all of our will, we will do it.

The most important element, however, in the development of a unified will is cooperation with the will of God, which daily prayer prepares us to do.

NOTES

1   John F. Harvey, O.S.F.S., *The Moral Theology of the Confessions* (Washington, D.C.: Catholic University of America, 1951), pp. 63-64. This book fully covers the ideas presented in this chapter. Specific references are limited for lack of space.

2   Ibid.

3   *The Confessions of St. Augustine*, trans. Sir Tobie Matthew, rev. Dom Roger Huddleston [1923] (London: Fontana, 1963), 8, 1, 1.

4   Harvey, *Moral Theology*, pp. 97-98.

5   *Confessions*, 7, 21, 27.

6   Ibid., 8, 5, 10.

7   Ibid., 8, 8, 19.

8   Ibid., 8, 8, 20.

9   Ibid. *Non igitur monstrum partim velle, partim nolle, sed aegritudo animi est.*

10   Ibid., 8, 9, 21.

11   Rudolph Allers, *Self Improvement* (New York: Benzinger, 1939), pp.13-15. Another book on the purpose of life based on Sacred Scripture is Rick Warren's *The Purpose-Driven Life* (Grand Rapids, MI: Zondervan, 2002). Highly recommended.

12   *Confessions*, 9, 1, 1.

13   Ibid., 8, 10, 22; also 7, 3, 5; 1, 7, 11-12.

14   Ibid., 8, 5, 10.

15   Patrick Carnes, *Contrary to Love: Helping the Sex Addict* (Minneapolis: Hazelden, 1994); Gerald G. May, *Addiction & Grace* (San Francisco: Harper, 1991).

CHAPTER 8

Norms for Admission to Seminaries and Holy Orders

1. **What is the purpose of the 2005 Vatican document Instruction Concerning the Criteria for the Discernment of Vocations with Regard to Persons with Homosexual Tendencies in View of Their Admission to the Seminary and to Holy Orders? Didn't the prefect of the Congregation for Catholic Education, Zenon Cardinal Grocholewski, say that there is nothing new in this document?**

While it is true that there are a number of Vatican documents that have dealt with the criteria for the discernment of a vocation to the priesthood, the authors found it necessary to reaffirm the norms.

2. **Why was it necessary to reaffirm these norms?**

In the prevailing atmosphere of many liberal seminaries, the erroneous notion has spread that a homosexual inclination is just as natural as a heterosexual one. In short, the instruction clears the air of false views concerning the matter, particularly the attitude that same-sex tendencies are no problem because, after all, heterosexual candidates also have to be chaste. This document will help bishops, major superiors, rectors, spiritual directors, and others authorized to make judgments concerning the suitability of candidates for admission to the seminary and to Holy Orders.

3. **What norms are presented to bishops, seminary rectors, and spiritual directors as aids in the process of discernment for admission of men with same-sex attraction?**

There are two types of norms: the psychological-spiritual and the moral-pastoral. The psychological-spiritual norms include affective maturity and spiritual fatherhood, whereas the moral-pastoral include homosexual activity, deep-seated homosexual inclinations, and an attitude which regards homosexual activity as a natural alternative for persons with same-sex attraction (SSA). Each category needs some explanation.

The first psychological norm is affective maturity, which means that the man possesses an emotional balance in which his emotions are subject to reason and will. Very often, persons with SSA are not emotionally balanced, tending to act like teenagers. They tend to have a hostile ambivalence toward members of their own sex which easily turns into undue attachment to a person of the same sex. A mature attitude would require that one be able to relate well to either sex. Correlative to affective maturity is spiritual fatherhood. It is said by some writers that men with SSA are not capable of spiritual fatherhood. From pastoral experience, however, I have known many persons with SSA who have been able to transcend this form of immaturity to become spiritual fathers to others.

4. **Speaking of psychological-spiritual norms, what is the relationship between affective maturity and the work of the Holy Spirit in a candidate to the priesthood?**

Affective maturity is concerned with the ability of the individual to bring his emotions in line with his reasoning and volitional powers. Once this is achieved with the help of the Holy Spirit, the candidate is open to the guidance of the same Spirit, who will form him into the image of Christ. In the words of the Vatican document, "By means of the Sacrament of Orders, the Holy Spirit configures the candidate to Jesus Christ in a new and specific way: the priest, in fact, sacramentally represents Christ, the head, shepherd, and spouse of the Church" (no. 1). This transformation, which takes many years, gives the priest spiritual maturity in serving Christ and His Church.

5. **Turning now to the moral-pastoral norms—which forbid homosexual activity, deeply rooted homosexual tendencies, and advocacy of a "gay" culture—what does the document mean by "homosexual activity"?**

It seems that the term usually means habitual homosexual activity, i.e., habitual sexual acts with a person of one's own sex. However, it can also mean one fully deliberate act of homosexuality immediately before the time when the candidate seeks to enter the seminary. Some would argue that if a person has practiced chastity for a significant time after an original failing, he would not fall under this category. (A more complete explanation of this question is offered in the answer to question six.)

6.   Are you saying, then, that an isolated homosexual act by a seminarian should *not* result in his being asked to leave the seminary?

No. I am saying that one deliberate homosexual act *is* a sufficient reason to request a seminarian to leave the seminary. If, however, it were an act of rape, the seminarian victim would be encouraged to remain in the seminary. Whether the person involved in an isolated act could return after three years of chaste living is a matter of debate. If a person has lived chastely for such a period, I would be inclined to consider his readmission, provided there is no other obstacle. This said, I submit my opinion to the Congregation for the Doctrine of the Faith.

7.   How does one explain deeply rooted homosexual tendencies?

There is little agreement on the explanation of "deeply rooted homosexual tendencies." I have shared my view with Dr. Richard Fitzgibbons, a psychiatrist in the Philadelphia area who has extensive experience working with persons with SSA, and we agree that one can discern such deeply-rooted tendencies when a person with same-sex attraction is either habitually or addictively engaged in homosexual acts or in the struggle against them. One must distinguish between a habit and an addiction. A bad moral habit implies that one still retains a measure of freedom, while an addiction means a loss of freedom with regard to a specific act. "Deeply rooted" covers both such habits and addictions. Persons so afflicted do not belong in a seminary, but they may be able to break such habits or addictions through individual therapy, participation in support systems like Courage, and constant prayer. Dr. Fitzgibbons and I have seen radical changes.

In the various moral and pastoral discussions of "deeply rooted" tendencies, there is little mention of the basic insight of Elizabeth Moberly—that in working with a person with same-sex attraction, one discovers that the person has a gender-identity problem rather than a sexual-genital one.[1] When the person understands the difference between his gender-identity problem and temptations to sexual-genital acts, he will be able to move away from such acts.

8. **The document says that those who support the gay culture should not be admitted to a Catholic seminary. Why is this necessary?**

Besides those who engage in homosexual activity and have deeply rooted same-sex attractions, a third group of candidates who should not be admitted to the seminary or to the priesthood are those who "support the so-called gay culture." It is necessary to define "gay culture." It is a philosophy of life which advocates homosexual behavior as a lawful alternative to the state of marriage. This philosophy holds that homosexual activity is natural and that one may look forward to finding a life partner. It also advocates that such sexual unions should have the same privileges as traditional marriage. If a candidate for the priesthood holds this view, he should not be ordained. Even heterosexual candidates who support the "gay culture" should not be ordained because they would mislead others, particularly persons with same-sex attraction.

9. **How does same-sex attraction hinder one's relationships to other men and women?**

To understand the difficulties faced by persons with same-sex attraction, it is helpful to appreciate that the natural attraction of man toward woman and woman toward man is the basis for the institution of marriage in every culture. The person with same-sex attraction generally lacks this natural attraction to the other sex, and he is also uneasy toward members of his own sex. Before he is brainwashed by gay propaganda, he may perceive that sexual actions with his own sex are immoral. In short, SSA is a deficit, affecting the person's relationships to other men and women. In seminarians, for example, it finds expression in resentment of the authority of the rector and in fear of competition from other candidates. In other cases, one finds a fear of women related to his earlier relationship with his mother; just as frequently, the candidate is resentful of the authority of his father. It is really hostile detachment from his father. Many women with SSA have also felt hostility toward their fathers.

10. Are homosexual tendencies transitory in some persons?

The document refers to one who is still in adolescence as an example of transitory homosexual tendencies. It is a good example but not the only one. The document goes on to say that the person must have clearly overcome these tendencies "at least three years before ordination to the diaconate" (no. 2). This would seem to refer to an adolescent already in the seminary. He would probably need an evaluation by a reliable psychiatrist or psychologist to discover whether his same-sex attraction is no longer deeply rooted and whether he has been chaste during this period.

The document, however, does not address the question of an adult person with SSA who has remained chaste while practicing chastity of the heart through prayer.

Both spiritual directors and Catholic therapists have encountered such persons. I believe that such individuals should have the opportunity to enter a seminary with the hope of subsequent ordination. They will need to be monitored by both a spiritual director and a therapist.

I believe that we need additional study of same-sex tendencies in adolescent seminarians. Spiritual directors, Catholic therapists, and moral theologians need to integrate their findings in this area.

11. What are the two inseparable elements found in every priestly vocation?

These two elements are: 1) a vocation is a free gift of God; and 2) it involves the responsible liberty of the man aspiring to the priesthood. On this subject, the document states: "A vocation is a gift of Divine Grace, received through the Church, in the Church and for the service of the Church" (no. 3). The candidate responds freely to the call of God in love. The desire to become a priest is not enough. There is no "right" to be ordained to the priesthood. It is the duty of the Church to discern the qualifications of one who wishes to enter a seminary and to spell out the necessary requirements for priestly ordination (no. 3).

12. What does the document say about the formation of seminarians for the priesthood?

After describing the requisite qualifications for admission to the seminary, the document addresses bishops, major superiors, rectors, and spiritual directors concerning their responsibility for the continued personal formation of the seminarians. This formation "must distinctly articulate, in an essentially complementarity manner, the four dimensions of formation: human, spiritual, intellectual, and pastoral" (no. 3). The document stresses that the human dimension of formation is the most important because it forms the foundation of the intellectual, spiritual, and pastoral dimensions.

I understand human foundation to refer to: a) a grounding in the reality that the human being is a body-person with intelligence, free will, and emotions, and with the power to control these emotions. This body-person understanding includes the complementarity of man and woman; b) an adequate intellectual capacity; and c) freedom from emotional disorders that hinder the free exercise of the will. I would place same-sex attraction under emotional disorders in the area of sexuality. With reference to the diaconate and priesthood, the document states that the candidate must have achieved "affective maturity" (no. 3).

13. How do seminary rectors and spiritual directors in seminaries discern that a candidate has achieved affective maturity?

I believe that the candidate has achieved affective maturity when he has learned through self-examination and prayer to place his intelligence and free will above his emotions. For example, feelings of self-pity, anger, resentment of authority, and inferiority are now under the control of deeply rooted chastity, or chastity of the heart. Affective maturity leads to spiritual fatherhood. Such a person comes across as well balanced.

14. But some persons come across as well balanced who aren't. How do rectors and spiritual directors tell the difference between a man who has achieved affective

maturity and a man who has only buried his emotions under an appearance of maturity?

There is probably no adequate answer to this question. From my forty years in spiritual direction in the seminary, I would say that the rector or superior in the external forum and spiritual directors in the internal forum can usually discern those with deep emotional problems and realize they need both spiritual and psychological help. Oftentimes, external behavior is noted by both the rector or superior and the seminary faculty.

15. Who is ultimately responsible for the ordination of a candidate to the priesthood?

The diocesan bishop or the major superior of a religious male congregation or order is ultimately responsible. They, in turn, charge seminary rectors and spiritual directors to discern the suitability for the priesthood of each seminarian. I use the term "ultimately" with regard to the bishop or major superior because they make the final decision and, in case of serious doubt, they are bound to deny ordination to a seminarian in favor of the common good of the Church.

The rector of the seminary, after consultation with the faculty, must make a decision with regard to the fitness of each seminarian for the priesthood. Finally, the spiritual director has an important role in the process of discernment; he works in the internal forum of conscience and is "bound to secrecy" (no. 3). But, like the rector, the spiritual director has a grave obligation to discern the suitability of the seminarians he directs. Representing the Church in the internal forum, he must find in the candidate the practice of priestly chastity as well as "the affective maturity that is characteristic of the priest" (no. 3). The spiritual director needs to ascertain the personal traits of the seminarian, who must meet with him regularly.

There is good reason for such intense inquiry in order to ascertain that the candidate does not present any sexual issues that are incompatible with the priesthood (see no. 3). Such issues would include habitual masturbation and addiction to pornography.

If the person with such issues were willing to leave the seminary until he has recovered from habitual masturbation and/or the use of pornography, he may be given the opportunity to renew his path to the priesthood. I would suggest a waiting period of about three years. If, however, the seminarian "practices homosexuality" or presents "profoundly deep-seated homosexual tendencies, his spiritual director as well as his confessor have the duty to dissuade him in conscience from proceeding towards ordination" (no. 3).

The document acknowledges that the candidate himself "has the first responsibility for his own formation" (no. 3). In a spirit of faith, he must submit his judgment to those representing the Church—"the bishop who calls to orders," the seminary rector, his spiritual director, and the faculty.

The document adds that it would be gravely dishonest for a candidate "to hide his own homosexuality in order to proceed, despite everything, towards ordination" (section 3). Such an attitude should not be found in one "called to serve Christ and His Church in the ministerial priesthood" (section 3).

The concluding statement of the document sums up its main purpose:

> Let bishops, episcopal conferences and major superiors look to see that the constant norms of this Instruction be faithfully observed for the good of the candidates themselves and to guarantee that the Church always has suitable priests who are true shepherds according to the heart of Christ (no. 3).

16. **Do you believe that this document will be helpful to American seminary rectors and spiritual directors?**

Yes, I believe it will be helpful in several ways:

1. It offers fresh perspective to bishops, rectors, spiritual directors, faculty, and seminarians. Issues which previously were looked upon as controversial are now settled by the document—for example, that it is gravely sinful to hide your same-sex attraction from the proper authorities.

2. It states clearly the responsibility of bishops and rectors in the external forum, while upholding the necessity of confidentiality by spiritual directors.

3. It admonishes spiritual directors to dissuade seminarians whom they judge to be lacking the qualities necessary for the priesthood to leave the seminary. This is done in confidentiality.

4. It makes a distinction between same-sex attraction and homosexual behavior.

5. It makes a distinction between deeply rooted homosexual tendencies and those that are not deeply-rooted. With regard to this distinction, it is advisable that

bishops seek guidance from professionals regarding the empirical evidence concerning variations of the intensity of such tendencies.

17. Would you like to add some further comments on the document?

Yes, I would. From a careful reading of this document I see the need for close cooperation among Catholic psychiatrists and psychologists, moral theologians, and seminary rectors, faculty, and spiritual directors.

In its May 2002 *Open Letter to the Bishops*, the Catholic Medical Association found "an enormous amount of misinformation about the nature, origins and treatment of homosexuality/SSA" among clergy and laity. This remains true today. Reading through a number of Internet articles on the document during late November and December of 2005, I noticed confusion concerning the phrase "deeply rooted homosexual tendencies." Some understood this phrase to mean *all* same-sex attractions; others wanted to see the term explained by Catholic therapists loyal to the Church. To be sure, the document makes a clear distinction between same-sex attraction as found in an adolescent (something presumably *temporary*) and deeply rooted same-sex attraction in an adult. The very use of the term "deeply rooted" same-sex attraction indicates that in some persons such attraction is not deeply rooted. In many years of pastoral work, I have seen variations in the intensity of same-sex attraction in the persons I have counseled. Dr. Richard Fitzgibbons makes the point that not only do men with SSA differ with regard to the strength of their same-sex attraction but that adult persons can reduce the strength of this attraction through therapy, group support, and prayer.

In reparative therapy, as practiced by the National Association for Research and Therapy of Homosexuality (NARTH), one finds plentiful evidence that homosexual tendencies can be reduced, and in some instances, eliminated. (See Dr. Robert Spitzer's statement in chapter 2.) In light of these developments, it would be helpful for persons whose responsibility it is to interpret the norms of this document to consult with the NARTH organization as well as with psychiatrists and psychologists who have a deep understanding of the sources of homosexual behavior.

---

[1] Elizabeth Moberly, *Psychogenesis* (Cambridge, England: Cambridge University Press, 1984). See chapter one.

CHAPTER 9

Courage, Encourage, and the Twelve Steps

Father, could you tell us more about Courage, Encourage, and the place of the Twelve Step Program in group meetings?

Yes. I will begin with the origin and purpose of Courage. Courage is a spiritual support group of men and women with same-sex attraction who desire to live chaste lives in accord with authentic Catholic teaching. The best way to elaborate on the significance of Courage is to describe its Five Goals. These goals were composed in the early 1980s by its founding members and are read at every meeting.

The Five Goals of Courage

1. To live chaste lives in accordance with the Roman Catholic Church's teachings on homosexuality.

2. To dedicate our entire lives to Christ through service to others, spiritual reading, prayer, meditation, individual spiritual direction, frequent attendance at Mass, and the frequent reception of the sacraments of Reconciliation and of the Holy Eucharist.

3. To foster a spirit of fellowship in which we may share with one another our thoughts and our experiences and to ensure that none of us will have to face the problems of homosexuality alone.

4. To be mindful of the truth that chaste friendships are not only possible but necessary in chaste
Christian life, and to encourage one another in
forming and sustaining them.

5. To live lives that may serve as good examples to
others.[1]

When one desires to join Courage, he or she must be willing
to accept the Five Goals, which serve as a screening test. The
practice of the first goal requires a docile heart willing to
go against the hedonism of our culture. It leaves no room
for negotiating with the views of the gay movement.

The second goal is concerned with one's prayer life. All
spiritual exercises are meant to lead to an interior way of
prayer, and the interior life of prayer leads one to a closer
union with Jesus Christ. The center of the interior life of
prayer is the daily practice of meditation. Learning how
to pray with the heart is the work of a lifetime. It leads
to a full-hearted chastity—that is, chastity of the heart or
interior chastity.

The third goal involves coming together to share our
experiences and to discover a sense of solidarity with other
members of Courage; this is the center of Courage meetings.
The meetings can be a great haven of encouragement
or they can become a dreary place where there is no real
guidance to challenge the lives of its members due to lack
of leadership and the absence of a vibrant prayer life. In
the latter situation, the group usually disintegrates and
disappears.[2]

For this reason, I want to explain the characteristics which
should make our meetings gatherings of encouragement:

- Every meeting must have a plan. The *Courage Handbook* gives discussion of the Twelve Steps a preferential place, that is to say, that the discussion of one of the Steps is the usual subject of a Courage meeting. The plan may also include testimonials, guest speakers on theology and psychology, and the Holy Sacrifice of the Mass.

- The leader of the group (either a priest or layperson) begins and ends meetings on time.

- The leader selects someone to present a topic at the following meeting.

- The leader gives everyone a chance to speak, while not allowing one member to dominate a meeting.

- Every meeting begins and ends with prayer.

- The members are encouraged to have some kind of informal social at the end of a meeting and to be in touch with each other between meetings, particularly at holiday times. It is important that we have good meetings where individuals can speak from the heart, knowing that they will be respected and supported by the group and that their confidences will be kept. Indeed, at the first meeting with new members, we emphasize that we must keep confidentiality and anonymity "as though a stole were around our neck."

Chapter 6 discusses in detail the fourth goal, the importance of chaste friendships. The fifth goal, to give good example to others, is best exemplified by the Courage videos *Portraits of Courage: Part I—Into the Light* and *Part II*

—*The Cry of the Faithful*, in which ten individuals with same-sex attraction publicly witness that chastity is possible for those with SSA.[3]

Courage does not consider the recovery of one's natural heterosexual orientation as one of its goals. Early in the history of Courage, some members, impressed by several Protestant groups whose primary objective was to help people recover from their homosexual condition, tried to convince the 1990 Philadelphia Conference that Courage should make the recovery of one's natural heterosexual inclination its sixth goal. The members present at the conference declined to do so, suggesting instead that those desiring to recover from same-sex attraction should seek help from a reliable therapist or from other groups whose mission is to help individuals in this regard. It was also requested that the 1991 Conference should focus on the Five Goals of Courage with primary emphasis on the virtue of chastity.

Recently, Courage has received requests from Catholic, Protestant, and Jewish leaders, indicating their desire to work with the organization on therapeutic methods designed to foster heterosexual development. As the director of Courage, I have proposed a different plan based on the Five Goals, along with the Twelve Steps adapted from Alcoholics Anonymous (AA), as means of advancement in virtue.[4] If a Courage member desires therapy, he may seek it in one of the professional agencies or from individual doctors who specialize in such therapy. The National Association for Research and Therapy of Homosexuality (NARTH) recommends therapists throughout the country to assist those who wish to come out of the condition.[5] Courage holds that any individual is free to make the effort to move away from same-sex attraction. There are many excellent therapeutic programs available throughout the United States.[6]

Hopefully, in the future, Courage will have sufficient funds to pay for professional therapy for those who are unable to afford it. Meanwhile, the work of Courage leaders is basically moral counseling and spiritual direction. Leaders themselves need to present a clear image of the purpose of Courage—to teach the members how to practice interior chastity, or chastity of the heart. But no one is capable of chastity of the heart unless he spends time in daily meditation, which is best described as prayer of the heart. As the spiritual adage goes, *Cor ad cor loquitur,* "heart speaks to heart."

Let us turn now to how Courage meetings profit from the Twelve Steps, as well as our manner of prayer and the kind of moral counseling and spiritual direction that flow from well-run meetings. With the formal permission of Alcoholics Anonymous, Courage has adapted the Twelve Steps, modifying only the wording of Step One: "We admitted that we were powerless over homosexuality, and our lives had become unmanageable."[7]

We continue to plan our meetings around the Twelve Steps because they have proven to be beneficial for members. However, as indicated in the *Courage Handbook,* meetings may also be planned around the presentation of a guest speaker, a member's testimonial, useful readings, and the celebration of the Mass. I ask new leaders of Courage to emphasize the Five Goals and the Twelve Steps as the norm in their meetings.

The value of the Twelve Steps is that they help keep the discussion on track. Each step is concerned with one or more virtues, and we can see a correlation of the steps with St. Francis de Sales' teachings in the third part of *Introduction to the Devout Life*. Step One, for example, is an acknowledgment of one's powerlessness over same-sex attractions, and the corresponding virtue is humility.[8] The difficulty which many experience with the steps, however, is a failure to apply them to oneself, while trying to apply them to others; they call us to take action and focus on ourselves as persons.

In a good session, the presenter applies the step under consideration to himself, relating his personal response of feelings of helplessness to the other members of the group, as noted above in Step One. In so doing he is communicating with others in the group. This may lead to other members identifying with the feelings of the presenter. As they express their own feelings, they have a sense of being a part of the group. They know that they can come back to other meetings and feel at home in the group.

There are those, however, who think that the Twelve Steps are not spiritual enough. In truth, Step One is a profound act of humility. Turning to a Power greater than oneself is, at first, an act of hope in the power of the group, which through divine grace can become the biblical virtue of hope. Step Three says: "We made a decision to turn our will and our lives over to the care of God as we understood Him." This is a profound surrender to the mysterious providence of God. Understood properly, the steps are rooted in the spiritual order.

What is needed in the Catholic concept of Courage is the integration of the Twelve Steps of AA with the prayer dimension of the Courage meeting. Individuals frequently refer to Courage as a "Twelve Step Outfit." It is far more than that. It is a form of spiritual direction.[9] The reading of the Five Goals, combined with a distinctly Catholic program of spirituality, indicates that Courage is an official ministry of the Roman Catholic Church, as approved by Cardinal Lopez Trujillo, President, Pontifical Council for the Family, on July 7, 1994.

In practice, the Twelve Steps are one of the means by which the individual member of Courage achieves chastity. Step One is a loving acknowledgment of our powerlessness before God and our willingness to seek help through the Courage group. As the individual and the group work through the successive steps, they are led to trust in God, to look honestly at failings and talents, and to make amends, thus developing a more spiritual life while reaching out to others.

Some Courage groups have failed to thrive and have even fallen apart. I believe there are several reasons for this:

1. The leader, whether clergy or lay, fails to conduct the type of meetings which motivate members to come back, e.g., allowing the discussion period to turn into a monologue by the leader or by one of the members.

2. Everyone present does not have an opportunity to speak.

3. On more than one occasion, members hear from the leader remarks which are ambivalent, if not erroneous.

4. The leader does not focus on the Twelve Steps (or on other matters of equivalent value) or is often absent. A meeting may sometimes continue in spite of these difficulties, but with fewer attending.

5. Some members become discouraged in their efforts to be chaste, often without discussing these difficulties with the group leader. As a result, they may leave Courage because they believe that Courage is not doing enough to help them.

6. Some persons stop attending meetings because their group does not use the Twelve Steps, focusing instead on reviewing books or discussing issues that do not refer directly to the members' needs.

By way of contrast, in well-run Courage meetings, people come to know themselves better and come closer to God by sharing with the group. Meetings in which the leader comes prepared, and where the person chosen to make a presentation is equally prepared, tend to thrive and increase in numbers.

Several priest leaders with wonderful backgrounds in clinical pastoral practice conduct insightful meetings. Courage priests willingly hear confessions after meetings. In some areas there is no priest at the Courage meeting, but generally members find supportive priests nearby.

Prayer at Courage Meetings

Each group decides on its opening prayers, followed by the reading of the Five Goals. Usually meetings close with the *Memorare*, although many groups first have prayers of petition and thanksgiving. Prayers close the formal meeting. If possible, a brief social takes place, often in a diner nearby. Such socials help newcomers immensely. There is another kind of prayer stressed in Goal Two, namely, meditation, which is explained in chapter ten on spiritual direction.

The Origin and Purpose of Encourage

In the early 1990s, several chapters of Courage in the Northeast began to form groups of parents who have sons or daughters with same-sex attraction. These groups operated under a variety of names until the annual Courage Conference of 1992 in Toronto, when the name Encourage was adopted.

The purpose of Encourage is to give faithful witness to Catholic teaching on sexual morality, while helping its members find a deeper spiritual life. Over the past fifteen years, I have had many conversations with parents, empathizing with their disappointment and deep fear concerning the salvation of the souls of their children. They tend to blame the condition of their son or daughter on themselves. They ask, "Why did God allow this to happen to me?" I try to help them accept the mysterious will of God in their lives.

In the words of Dr. John Nace, former president of the Philadelphia Encourage chapter:

> Encourage differs from other Christian ministries of a similar
> purpose in that it does not embrace the *necessity* of a homosex-
> ual loved one's changing sexual orientation... *Encourage* works
> primarily to cultivate a supportive, accepting environment in
> which the more immediate goals of fostering personal chas-
> tity and sexual abstinence can be valued within the context of
> a broadly Christian appreciation of human experience.[10]

The belief that a change in orientation is not a necessity is
strongly held by Courage. Parents often want to "fix things"
or "make things right." This can be a false hope which does
not take into consideration the condition and capability of
their son or daughter. I might add that other organizations
actually seek to have the parents approve the homosexual
lifestyle.[11] Instead, both Courage and Encourage approve
the method of helping the individual himself take the
initiative in reducing the power of same- sex attraction.
In adopting the name Encourage, the group accepted as
well the goals of Courage from which it came.

The Four Goals of Encourage

1. To promote a spirit of compassion and acceptance
   among the members so that they may share with
   one another their thoughts and experiences and
   so ensure that no one will have to face the problems of homosexual loved ones alone.

2. To foster the practice of service to others, spiritual
   reading, prayer, meditation, individual spiritual
   direction, frequent attendance at Mass, and the
   frequent reception of the sacraments of reconciliation and the Holy Eucharist.

3. To encourage loved ones in the development of
   chaste friendships.

4. To witness by good example to others who have homosexual loved ones.

Father Don Timone, who has led an Encourage group in upstate New York, has suggested the following goals for these parents and friends of Courage: 1) to help members themselves grow spiritually through developing a vital relationship with the Lord Jesus Christ, as authentically taught in Catholic Tradition; 2) to enable members to gain a deeper understanding of the needs, problems, and issues experienced by men and women with same-sex attraction; 3) to assist other parents and friends to reach out with compassion and truth to their loved ones with same-sex attraction.

A note on publicity: *Encourage members desire privacy* concerning their son or daughter, while they also seek support from other members. They depend upon discreet publicity from parish bulletins or the diocesan newspaper to inform other parents who might want to join the local Encourage group. Actually, the best publicity Encourage receives is at the annual Courage Conference, which attracts several hundred persons from all parts of the world. Often, after the annual conference parents call the Courage central office in New York, desiring to start an Encourage (and, hopefully, a Courage) group. Members of Encourage regularly attend the annual Courage conferences, deriving great consolation from socializing with Courage leaders and members. In chapter thirteen, Robert and Susan Cavera, who have become the international leaders of Encourage, present an updated picture of their apostolate.

NOTES

1   *Courage Handbook*, 1995 edition. See the Courage website, www. couragerc.net.

2   *Handbook*, pp. 5-8.

3   Copies of the Courage videos are available from the Courage central office in New York by calling 1-866-232-4278.

4   The Twelve Steps are reprinted in this section by permission of Alcoholics Anonymous World Services, 475 Riverside Drive, New York, NY 10115. (212) 870-3400. Their website is www. alcoholics-anonymous.org. (Permission to reprint and adapt the Twelve Steps in no way implies that AA is in any way affiliated with Courage.) See *Courage Handbook*, p. 7.

5   NARTH, 16633 Ventura Blvd., Suite 1340, Encino, CA 91436-1801. (818) 789-4440. www.narth.com.

6   Just to name a few: Dr. Joseph Nicolosi of Thomas Aquinas Institute, Encino, California; Dr. Richard Fitzgibbons of Comprehensive Psychological Services, Conshohocken, Pennsylvania; Regeneration of Baltimore, Maryland; and Andy Comisky, Desert Streams Ministry Program, Anaheim, California.

7   See note 4.

8   *Devout Life*, pt. 3, ch. 5, on interior humility.

9   Barbara Breaud, O.Carm, "The 12 Steps and St. John of the Cross," *Spiritual Life* 51, no. 1 (Spring 2005): pp. 47-54. She has led therapy groups of religious and clergy for twelve years.

10   John Nace, "Encourage," *The Family*, November 1993, pp. 18-19.

11   See Harvey, *The Truth about Homosexuality*, pp. 69-122.

CHAPTER 10

Spiritual Direction

Father, in your decades of pastoral ministry, you have helped many men and women with same-sex attraction come closer to Christ. Could you share what helps those you guide?

My response to the above question is that the principles I have taken from St. Francis de Sales apply equally to men and women with same-sex attraction. As an Oblate of St. Francis de Sales, I follow St. Francis' method of spiritual direction, as exemplified in his classic work *Introduction to the Devout Life*.[1] Through a careful reading of this volume, the reader can enter into his spirit of gentleness, firmness, and humility. As Cardinal Wiseman puts it, you can go through all his writings and "find no bitterness."[2] St. Francis' writings are full of encouragement for all Christians, including persons with same-sex attraction. Many use the *Devout Life* as their form of spiritual direction, given that spiritual directors are very difficult to find in our day. I shall turn now to the method and content of the book.

In Part I, St. Francis concentrates on the purification of the affections: "So also a soul that hopes for the honor of being made spouse of the Son of God must 'put off the old man and put on the new' by forsaking sin and removing and cutting away whatever obstructs union with God. For us the beginning of good health is to be purged of our sinful tendencies."[3] This purification of the affections is a great aid to the practice of chastity.

After explaining the first purgation from mortal sin, St. Francis suggests ten meditations as means of further purgation from affection for sin. These include our creation, destiny, personal gifts, sin, death, and our final goal. St. Francis maintains that affections for lust, pride, and greed block our spiritual progress.

In Part II, St. Francis explains the importance of meditation or prayer of the heart. In my pastoral guidance of Courage members I find many who do not know how to meditate. In my opinion, their struggles with temptations to lust would be easier (though not necessarily easy) if they were to spend a period of time in meditation every day. Of course, meditation has many other benefits, such as peace of soul and a well-ordered life of prayer with Jesus Christ.

St. Francis actually teaches people how to pray with the heart. In his instructions he stresses the importance of the emotions, or affections. He says that if one is dwelling upon a truth of Faith, such as the Passion of Christ, and one's affections are moved, one should dwell upon the scene of Christ's sufferings. Perhaps an example of Francis' method of meditation is helpful:

1. Invoke the Presence of God.

2. Make reflections on the agony of Christ in the garden: He had been abandoned by His disciples, and fearing His imminent suffering and death, He addressed His Father, "Father, if thou art willing, remove this cup from me; nevertheless not my will, but thine, be done" (Lk 22:42). In His human nature Christ recoiled at the thought of

the passion, but by divine grace He accepted His Father's will.

3. Let your affections be moved by the image of the Suffering Christ. He suffered for me in Gethsemane. How great was His suffering. May I learn to carry the crosses of loneliness, of feeling abandoned by friends, and of depression.

4. From these and similar sentiments, one forms a specific resolution; for example, when I feel depressed or discouraged, I will think of Christ in the Garden, and I will find strength to accept my sickness and frustration.

5. As I finish this meditation, I will repeat these words of Christ, "My soul is very sorrowful, even to death" (Mk 14:34).

After teaching a person how to meditate, St. Francis has useful reflections on handling difficulties in the effort to meditate. He observes that very holy people have such trials. A recent example is the accident suffered by Father Benedict Groeschel, C.F.R. In Part IV, Francis mentions anxiety and sorrow (chapters 11 and 12).

There are other factors which make meditation difficult. These may include lack of rest, constant tensions at work, feelings of self-hatred, and abandonment. In such situations Francis recommends the use of brief prayers frequently during the day, for example: "My Jesus, Mercy" or "Sacred Heart of Jesus, I place my trust in Thee."

Again, I find in the *Spiritual Directory of the Oblates of St. Francis de Sales* a "Brief Preparation for the Day": 1) in a brief prayer, call on Almighty God; 2) reflect on what occurred during the previous day. Perhaps you expressed anger at a particular person for failing to carry out a certain task; 3) realize that you overreacted; 4) form a very specific resolution about how you will respond this day to a similar situation in which you may be provoked to anger; 5) make an aspiration recalling your need for patience. This brief reflection can take two minutes. Thus, in the first two parts of the *Devout Life* we see Francis focusing his spiritual direction on the art of prayer. I have used this wisdom in guiding members of Courage in the art of meditation. Francis leads us in Part III of the *Devout Life* to an exploration of the virtues we need to practice in our effort to follow Christ.

In using the Twelve Step Program, a Courage member is constantly trying to practice virtues, such as humility, chastity, patience, and hope. In this effort he will find insight from Part III of the *Devout Life*. First, Francis discusses the importance of deciding what are the virtues one needs in order to fulfill the duties of his state in life. Courage members will find helpful Francis' treatment of patience and the three degrees of humility.

Chapter 3 deals with patience. The saint writes: "Do not limit your patience to this or that kind of injury or affliction. Extend it universally to all those God will send you or let happen to you. Some men wish to suffer no tribulations, except those connected with honor, for example, or to be wounded and made a prisoner of war, persecuted for religion, or impoverished by some law suit which they lost. Such men do not love tribulation, but the honor that goes with it. The truly patient man and true servant of God bears up equally with tribulations accompanied by ignominy and those that bring honor."[4]

Many people with same-sex attraction indulge in self-pity, as Gerard van den Aardweg states in his writings. Chapter 3 from his book *On the Origins and Treatment of Homosexuality*, entitled "The Self-Pitying Child,"[5] can help such persons to overcome self-pity. So also does the teaching of St. Francis about the loving acceptance of self.

In chapter 4, St. Francis decribes the first degree of humility as the virtue of modesty; this is opposed to vainglory, the tendency to put oneself on a pedestal and to imagine oneself as superior to others. Francis desires that we look deeper into ourselves in order to practice interior humility. Before describing this deeper humility in chapter 5, Francis refers to the fear many have that they should not dwell on the particular graces God has shown them, "because they are afraid that this may arouse vainglory and self-complaisance. They deceive themselves in this. Since the true means to attain the love of God is consideration of His benefits, as the great Angelic Doctor states, the more we know about them, the more we shall love Him. As the particular benefits He has conferred on us affect us more powerfully than those we share with others, they must be considered more attentively."[6]

St. Francis adds that we need not fear that reflections on the special gifts God has given us will make us proud, "if only we remember this truth, that none of the good in us comes from ourselves."[7] Truly, when we lovingly accept the gifts of God, we thank God for the gifts. Thus, to be grateful is to be humble. Interior humility is then a loving acceptance of God's gifts to us individually, while acknowledging our dependence upon Him for the graces to do His will.

In chapter 6, St. Francis considers the most difficult form of humility, loving our own abjection. When in her *Magnificat* Mary says that because Our Lord "has regarded the humility of His handmaid, 'all generations will call her blessed,' she means that Our Lord has graciously looked down on her abjection, meanness and lowliness in order to heap graces and favors upon her."[8]

St. Francis, however, distinguishes between the virtue of humility and abjection. One can be abject and lowly without awareness of his condition; humility is true knowledge and voluntary acknowledgment of our own abjection. The term *abjection* is not easy to understand. Mary regarded herself as lowly before the glory of God, but grateful that God had called her to be the Mother of the Savior. "The chief point of such humility consists not only in willingly admitting our abject state, but in loving it and delighting in it. This must not be because of lack of courage and generosity, but in order to exalt God's majesty all the more and to hold our neighbor in higher esteem than ourselves."[9] Francis encourages us to practice the love of abjection out of love for Christ.

Indeed, the most powerful example of this virtue, loving our own abjection, is Jesus in His passion and death. The film *The Passion of the Christ* is a beautiful portrayal of Jesus practicing this virtue. Most of us find it very difficult to put this virtue into practice, but for those who have accepted humiliations in the name of Christ, it is a source of peace of heart. It is, nonetheless, a difficult virtue for most of us, yet one finds it in the lives of the saints who accepted various forms of humiliation and persecution as they were led by the spirit of God. It is an act of the highest part of our will motivated by the love of Christ. One sees it particularly in the mystics, in Saints Pio of Pietrelcina (Padre Pio), Faustina, Bernadette, Margaret Mary, Joan of Arc, and John of the Cross.

In chapter 8, "Gentleness Towards Others," St. Francis quotes the Gospel passage: "Learn from me, for I am meek and humble of heart, and you shall find rest for your souls" (Mt 11:29). Francis counsels us not to be angry at all, if that is possible. "Do not accept any pretext whatever for opening your heart's door to anger. St. James tells us positively and without reservation, the anger of man does not work the justice of God.[10] Francis quotes St. Augustine, who holds that it is better to deny entrance to just and reasonable anger than to admit it, no matter how small it is. Once anger is allowed in, it is driven out only with difficulty. It is nourished by a thousand false pretexts. There has never been an angry man who believed his anger was unjust.[11]

As one reflects upon the wisdom of St. Augustine and St. Francis, both of whom believed that we should not dwell on emotions of anger but pray to God to overcome such feelings, one realizes how right they were. For some of us, like myself, they become an inspiration to quickly rid ourselves of angry thoughts and feelings which one harbors at too great a price.

Many persons with same-sex attraction have anger without realizing how deeply that anger is buried within them. They need a counselor to help manage such anger, and they need to bring it to Christ in prayer after the manner of Leanne Payne in *The Broken Image*.[12] Payne treats the immaturity and insecurity in her patients with a program which integrates the psychological with the spiritual. This kind of therapy is described in the third chapter of *The*

Broken Image. In this way she helps to resolve their deep insecurity and their anger.[13]

Some of our best Courage meetings have dealt with various forms of anger in different persons: anger directed at self, parents, peers, siblings, priests, and God. Sometimes a Courage member, now aware of the anger within him, will go to a reliable clinical psychologist for insight into his heart. Steps Eight and Nine of AA consider the need to forgive, and the need to ask for forgiveness. It is noteworthy that the teaching of Francis on anger confirms the wisdom of the Twelve Steps.

In Chapter 9, St. Francis speaks of gentleness toward ourselves. Here he speaks to the whole Church, and I believe these words can be applied in a special way to persons wounded by same-sex attraction. Francis speaks about the way we beat ourselves down: "We must not fret over our own imperfections. Although reason requires that we should be displeased and sorry whenever we commit a fault, we must refrain from bitter, gloomy, spiteful, and emotional displeasure."[14] Francis explains how we allow anger to get out of control: "When overcome by anger, they become angry at being angry, disturbed at being disturbed, and vexed at being vexed. By such means they keep their hearts drenched and steeped in passion."[15]

These bitter feelings toward oneself are tinged with pride and are nothing more than exaggerated expressions of self-love. It is important that one learn to be gentle with oneself. This does not mean that one is careless, but simply that an individual does his best, and is not discouraged by mistakes and failures.

In his letters, St. Francis repeats the advice that one must be gentle with oneself on every occasion: "Lift up your heart again whenever it fails, but do so meekly by humbling yourself before God through knowledge of your own misery, and do not be surprised if you fall. It is no wonder that infirmity should be infirm, weakness weak, or misery wretched. Nevertheless, detest with all your powers the offense God has received from you and with great courage and confidence in his mercy return to the path of virtue you had forsaken."[16]

In chapter 10, St. Francis distinguishes between care and diligence on the one hand, and worry and anxiety on the other. "The angels take care for our salvation and are diligent to procure it, but they are not solicitous, worried, and anxious."[17] He desires that we rely solely on God's Providence through which alone we must look for success. He makes the point that worry disturbs reason and good judgment and "prevents us from doing well the very things we are worried about."[18]

In chapter 12, St. Francis notes the necessity of chastity and in chapter 13 he advises us how to preserve chastity: "Chastity depends on the heart for its source, but on the body as its subject. For this reason it may be lost both by the body's external senses and by thoughts and desires within the heart."[19]

In chapters 17 to 22, Francis speaks of three kinds of friendship: good, evil, and foolish ("fond loves"). These chapters are full of wisdom for Christians in every age. (In this book, friendship is treated in chapter 6. This chapter gives special attention to friendships among Courage members, discussing both benefits and boundaries.)

Throughout the rest of Part III St. Francis treats a variety of virtues and states of life. Particularly important with reference to the contemporary media culture are his chapters on speech (26-30). He shows the evil of destroying the reputation of persons through calumny and slander. The reader will enjoy chapter 36, which is entitled "We Must Preserve a Just and Reasonable Mind": "We are men solely because we possess reason, yet it is a rare thing to find men who are truly reasonable. Usually self-love leads us away from reason and directs us imperceptibly into countless small yet dangerous acts of injustice and iniquity, which, like the little foxes, spoken of in the *Canticle of Canticles,* destroy the vines."[20]

In Part IV, "Necessary Counsels Against the Most Frequent Temptations," St. Francis speaks of the importance of fortitude in overcoming the criticisms of the world. Always the teacher, he explains the difference between consent to temptation and resisting grave sins.[21]

St. Francis makes it clear that one may be subject to strong temptations and even feel them without consenting to them "as long as the temptation is displeasing to one's will, one does not sin."[22] In chapters 3 to 10, Francis gives examples that illustrate the difference between feeling temptation and giving consent to it, while encouraging the reader to pray in the midst of temptation.

In chapters 11 and 12, St. Francis discusses the dangers of anxiety and depression. He distinguishes carefully between anxiety and sadness. "Anxiety is not a simple temptation, but a source from which and by which many temptations arise, and for this reason I will say something concerning it. Sadness is merely the grief of mind we have because of an evil experienced contrary to our will. It may be external, like poverty; it may be internal, like discontent. When a person perceives that he suffered a certain evil, he may tend to dwell upon it."[23]

He may wish to escape from his sorrow. There is nothing wrong in wishing to escape from an evil. If he wishes to escape from troubles out of love for God, he will do so patiently and humbly, looking for deliverance "rather by God's Providence than [by his] own efforts, industry, or diligence. If [the soul] seeks deliverance because of self-love, then, as if success depended on itself rather than on God, it will excite and wear itself out in its search for a means of escape."[24]

If the soul does not succeed in the way it desires, it will become very anxious and impatient; then, instead of removing the evil, it makes it worse. In great anguish, the soul begins to lose courage and hope; it imagines the evil to be incurable. Thus, sadness, which was justified in the beginning, produces anxiety, and anxiety, in its turn, leads to more sadness. Francis sees all this as "extremely dangerous," leading him to say that "with the single exception of sin, anxiety is the greatest evil that can happen to a soul."[25]

As a spiritual director and a moral theologian, I have worked with such anxious people. It is necessary to put their minds at rest and to help them to reason calmly. Try gently to do one thing at a time.

St. Francis concludes his advice on anxiety with a suggestion: "If you can reveal the cause of your anxiety to your spiritual director, or to some faithful and devout friend, you may be assured that you will speedily find relief. To share your heart's grief with others...is the remedy of remedies."[26] In our culture anxious persons may gain much insight through reliable therapy and good spiritual direction.

In chapter 12, Francis explains the passage from St. Paul which distinguishes two kinds of sorrow: 1) that which is in accord with our salvation; and 2) that which is in accord with the world, leading to death.[27]

St. Francis points out that sorrow has only two good effects, repentance and compassion, and six evil effects, namely, anxiety, sloth, jealousy, envy, impatience, and wrath. The devil is engaged in the negative effects: "The enemy uses sorrow to set temptations before good men. Just as he tries to induce the sinner to rejoice in his sin, so also he tries to make the good person regret their virtues and good works...The evil one is pleased with sadness and melancholy, because he himself is sad and melancholy, and will be for all eternity. Hence he desires that everyone be like himself."[28]

Thus, Francis sees evil sorrow as very destructive of souls, taking away "all sweetness from the soul, and rendering it disabled and impotent in all its faculties. In a word, it is like a severe winter, which spoils all the beauty of the country and weakens all the animals."[29]

This leads him to suggest the following remedies: 1) In the words of St. James, "Is anyone among you suffering? Let him pray" (Jas 5:13); "O God of my heart, my joy and my hope"; 2) In moments of depression "oppose vigorously any tendency to sadness."[30] The enemy tries to make us weary of good works; 3) Occupy yourself with various *exterior* works. This keeps you from obsessing over the incident or person that has led to sadness; 4) Perform fervently external acts of devotion, even though you do not relish them, such as kissing a crucifix; 5) Receive the Holy Eucharist as often as possible; and 6) "Humbly and sincerely reveal to your confessor all the feelings, affections, and suggestions that proceed from your sadness."[31]

St. Francis believed that both anxiety and sadness, when persistent, gravely harm spiritual progress, often leading to discouragement and despair. He strongly recommends that the person in these emotional states seek regular guidance from a spiritual director. Nowadays similar counsel can be sought, if possible, from a qualified Catholic therapist. The concern of St. Francis for those afflicted with sadness and anxiety is understandable when one considers that he held that the following of Christ was a joyous journey to the Triune God.

St. Francis recommends that the aspirant to the devout life make a retreat each year. Part V of the *Devout Life* provides the reader with ample material for a private retreat. It could also be used in a directed retreat.

Having said all this, one needs to reflect upon what writers call "the spirit of St. Francis de Sales." Each religious order has a special spiritual gift: the Franciscans for poverty, the Dominicans for intellectual discourse, the Benedictines for stability, and the Carmelites for contemplation. The spirit of Francis de Sales is one of profound humility before God and of loving service to our neighbor. Francis himself said that such was the spirit of the Visitation Sisters, and the Oblates of St. Francis de Sales came from these sisters. A Visitation sister, Mother Mary de Sales Chappuis, persuaded the chaplain of the Visitation monastery in Troyes, France, to found a congregation of men to educate the youth of France in the Catholic faith in 1875. Today his spirit would be called upbeat in a very profound sense. As I have already said, his spirit is one of sweetness in which there is no place for bitterness or sarcasm. There are three virtues which best represent his spirit: profound humility, gentleness of heart, and sweetness in communicating with his neighbor.

So many Catholics want spiritual direction. This chapter illustrates the method of St. Francis de Sales. I hope it may lead readers, especially members of Courage, to use *Introduction to the Devout Life* as a guide in their spiritual life; it has helped me in my religious life.

NOTES

1 Francis de Sales, *Introduction to the Devout Life*, trans. John K. Ryan (New York: Doubleday, 1989).

2 *The Spiritual Conferences of St. Francis de Sales*, trans. Mackey-Quasquet (London: Burns and Washbourne, 1923), pp. xxxv-lxvii.

3 *Devout Life*, pt. 1, ch. 5.

4 Ibid., pt. 3, ch. 3.

5 Gerard van den Aardweg, *On the Origins and Treatment of Homosexuality* (New York: Praeger, 1986), p. 19.

6 *Devout Life*, pt. 3, ch. 5.

7 Ibid.

8 Ibid., pt. 3, ch. 6.

9 Ibid.

10 Ibid., pt. 3, ch. 8.

11 Ibid.

12 Leanne Payne, *The Broken Image* (Westchester, IL: Crossway Books, 1982), p. 19.

13 Harvey, *The Homosexual Person*, p. 194.

14 *Devout Life*, pt. III, ch. 9.

15 Ibid.

16 Ibid., pt. 3, conclusion of ch. 9.

17 Ibid., pt. 3, ch. 10.

18 Ibid.

19 Ibid., pt. 3, ch. 13.

20 Ibid., pt. 3, ch. 36.

21 Ibid., pt. 4, ch. 2 and 3.

22 Ibid., pt. 4, ch. 3.

23 Ibid., pt. 4, ch. 11.

24 Ibid.

25 Ibid.

26 Ibid.

27 Ibid., pt. 4, ch. 12. The text from St. Paul is 2 Corinthians 7:9-10 (NAB).

28 Ibid.

29 Ibid.

30 Ibid.

31 Ibid., pt. 4, ch. 12, p. 255.

CHAPTER 11

Other Organizations Seeking to Help Persons with Same-Sex Attraction

In addition to Courage, are there other organizations that offer help to people with same-sex attraction that you would recommend?

Yes, there are several that are members of the PATH coalition.

PATH:
Positive Alternatives to Homosexuality

PATH is a coalition of organizations who work with people with unwanted same-sex attraction (SSA). PATH helps persons with SSA realize their personal goals for change in two ways: 1) by developing their innate heterosexual potential, or 2) adopting a lifestyle as a single, non sexually active man or woman.

"Collectively, our organizations have worked with thousands of men and women who have found peace and fulfillment by resolving their SSA feelings in ways that are emotionally healing, gender affirming and in agreement with their deeply-held values and beliefs, and supportive of their individual life goals. Many have transitioned out of a homosexual identity and lifestyle, while others have avoided ever going fully into it. Some have married and had children of their own. Some have saved their existing marriages and families. Some have found fulfillment in living as a single man or woman, with no homosexual involvement."[1]

The above statement of PATH emphasizes that individuals with SSA can have positive alternatives to living a homosexual lifestyle. It places great value on a person's freedom to resist these feelings and to turn away from the seductive invitations of homosexual groups. Some also may choose to recover their natural heterosexual inclinations through the various alternatives to the homosexual lifestyle. PATH also provides information on positive alternatives to the homosexual lifestyle. Considering the tremendous pressure placed upon persons with SSA to embrace a gay manner of living, PATH "supports individual self-determination. Individuals conflicted over their same-sex attractions have the right to decide whether to seek counseling or therapy; what kind of counseling to seek; to be aware of all alternatives."[2]

Those who turn away from a homosexual lifestyle and choose to pursue alternatives to homosexuality deserve our compassion and respect. They should not be subjected to ridicule and marginalization. Mindful of hate-crime legislation in both Canada and the United States, PATH expresses its concern that "laws regarding hate-crimes and sexual orientation...may be construed to make it illegal to promote or even to speak about alternatives to homosexuality."[3]

Another concern of PATH is that its member organizations, including Courage, do not have access to public forums equally with gay organizations. For years now PFLAG, an organization of parents and relatives of persons with SSA who support the homosexual lifestyle, has had almost exclusive access to public television and public school systems. It will be difficult for PATH to change this situation; Courage is willing to be involved in this struggle.

JONAH:
Jews Offering New Alternatives to Homosexuality

JONAH is an international organization ministering to Jews with same-sex attraction with programs of reorientation therapy. Rabbi Menachum Schneerson was a leader in helping Jewish persons recover their natural heterosexual inclinations. He believed that "despite the misguided way of the past, everyone has the power to change their sexual orientation, foreshadowed by what is today known as 'reparative therapy.'"[4]

Through therapy and spirituality a person conflicted about homosexual desires can reclaim his wholeness and gender identity. Appropriate reorientation counseling can help a person with SSA to break down "old patterns of avoidance and defensive detachment from one's own sex."[5]

JONAH is an umbrella organization with a central office in Jersey City, New Jersey. It houses counseling rooms, a library and a staff. It is also the first Jewish organization to minister to those troubled by same-sex attraction and their families. JONAH maintains a confidential hotline and a staff of preapproved therapists and counselors for psychotherapy, religious counseling, and support groups.

Referring to seven as the classic Jewish number signifying wholeness, Arthur Goldberg, co-director of JONAH, lists seven items on the Journey to Wholeness : 1) the Lubavitcher Rebbe's Sicha, "On Healing Homosexuality";

2) *Our Stories: Testimonials by Jewish Recovered Homosexuals*;
3) "Root Problems, Homosexual Symptoms," found at
www.peoplecancatch.com; 4) "Definitions and Causes
of Same-Sex Attractions"; 5) "The Three Myths about
Homosexuality," discussion from the NARTH website; 6)
JONAH's Recommended Reading List: websites, books,
papers discussing same-sex attractions; 7) article from the
Jewish Voice and Opinion (Dec. 1999, vol. 13, no. 4). Goldberg
asks the reader to review the above information, and, if
interested, be in touch with JONAH for further help.·[6]

Evergreen International

Evergreen International is a nonprofit organization
affiliated with the Mormons (officially, the Church of
Jesus Christ of Latter-Day Saints). Its purpose is to help
persons with SSA to diminish same-sex attraction, and
to overcome homosexual behavior through therapy,
prayer, and group support. It is not a clinical therapy
program, but it emphasizes the value of therapy, prayer,
and group support, and recommends to persons in need
of professional therapy that they see clinical psychologists
and psychiatrists. Indeed, Evergreen International has such
professional resources available. They regard Jesus Christ
as a prophet and model of virtue but not as the Second
Person of the Holy Trinity. The majority of Evergreen
groups are located in the western United States, with a
large number in Utah, though there are also foundations
in Australia. Most Evergreen groups have no women,
except in Salt Lake City and Nashville.

Evergreen features the writings of A. Dean Byrd, particularly
Homosexuality and the Church of Jesus Christ, which argues
against biological determinism. It also uses the works

of Jason Parks, *Resolving Homosexual Problems—A Guide for LDS Men* and *Helping LDS Men Resolve their Homosexual Problems.*[7] Park's first book deals with the members of Evergreen, while his second helps relatives and friends of their families. As a guide to Evergreen, psychotherapist Richard Cohen has offered a great deal of insight.

International Healing Foundation

The International Healing Foundation (IHF), established in 1990 by psychotherapist Richard Cohen, is a nonprofit organization which has educated, counseled, and trained thousands of men, women, and adolescents over the past seventeen years. IHF seeks to help each man, woman, and child in healing from past and present wounds, and empower him or her with the understanding of one's value as a child of God.[8]

Having come to know Richard Cohen over the last decade, I admire the way in which he moved from being a person with SSA to becoming a therapist willing and able to help others in their efforts to recover their natural heterosexual inclinations.

Cohen's *Coming Out Straight* deals with causes of same-sex attraction and ways of healing such. He spends time on the process of moving from a homosexual condition to a heterosexual one. Cohen appears in the Courage video, *Portraits of Courage,* explaining how he was able to be reconciled with his father. It is a moving scene. The story of his childhood is chronicled in *Alfie's Home,* a book I have found to be very helpful in understanding the childhood of persons with SSA. I believe Richard Cohen's therapeutic tools and techniques are very helpful as well, and I recommend his work and that of the International Healing Foundation to members of Courage. Like hundreds of other therapists, Cohen belongs to NARTH, the National Association of Research and Therapy of Homosexuality.[9]

NARTH:
National Association for Research
and Therapy of Homosexuality

NARTH is a member of PATH and works closely with all PATH members. As an associate member, I have followed the development of this organization over the past decade or so. It is a great help to the Courage central office in New York. We often receive calls from persons with same-sex attraction or their parents, seeking to find a therapist who will help them reduce same-sex attraction, or with the help of prayer and group support, to recover their natural heterosexual inclinations. Our New York office has made many contacts with NARTH therapists in different parts of the country, and in this way we have been able to refer persons with SSA to trustworthy therapists. The *NARTH Bulletin* also keeps one up to date on scientific studies of reorientation therapy and other insights of NARTH therapists throughout the country. The *NARTH Bulletin* is published three times a year.[10]

In the December 2004 issue of the *NARTH Bulletin*, a former president of the American Psychological Association (APA) gave strong support to NARTH's mission statement concerning client self-determination. At its November 2004 Conference in Washington, D.C., Dr. Robert Perloff said: "I am pleased to see an organization such as NARTH that supports freedom to change."[11]

PFOX:
Parents and Friends of Ex-Gays

Several years ago I gave a workshop to PFOX members in northern Virginia.[12] In a welcome letter, CEO Regina Griggs states that PFOX follows the principles of PATH, summarized above. Parents and persons with SSA manifest unconditional love for one another. Parents can love their children unconditionally without approval of their behavior. Griggs points out that no one is born gay and that ex-gays are living proof that same-sex attraction does not have to be permanent. Individuals with SSA can and do make decisions to reduce the strength of SSA and, if possible, to eliminate them. On the PFOX website one finds the latest research on same-sex attractions, together with summaries of important leaders in this area; for example, Dr. Robert Perloff speaks of the right of the person with SSA to self-determination.

Dr. Warren Throckmorton, past president of the American Mental Health Counseling Association, says that sexual orientation is a socially constructed product of experiences and can therefore be modified; people who modify their orientation through therapy are known as ex-gays. Dr. Throckmorton has published research consistent with this view, making it clear that he contradicts the policies of major mental-health associations. His research suggests that homosexual orientation, once thought to be an unchanging mental trait, is actually flexible, "changing as the result of therapy for some, ministry for others, and spontaneously for others."[13]

Other researchers and leaders in reorientation therapy are mentioned by PFOX in a helpful bibliography. Despite all these positive outcomes, there is need to challenge the bias of public school systems, like that of Fairfax, Virginia, who do not grant equal access to organizations like PFOX.

Exodus

Exodus International is the largest Christian organization involved in helping the homosexual person to recover his or her natural heterosexual inclinations. In its early history, each group which sought membership in Exodus was attached to a specific Protestant Church; this umbrella organization later became both international and interdenominational.[14] It is international in that Exodus has ministered to groups all over the world. Many Catholics who desire to come out of the condition of homosexuality frequent the Exodus annual conference, which is attended by more than five hundred people from the United States and many other nations. They have many good speakers, and Catholics will find the sessions rewarding.

Courage members attending the Exodus annual conferences gain insight into the psychological nature of same-sex attraction, and, if desirous of reorientation therapy, will find psychologists and psychiatrists at the conference to help them. At the same time these Catholics continue to share in the rich sacramental dimension of the Catholic Church; they also receive from the Church a clear understanding of the supernatural virtue of chastity. There is no conflict, then, between the purpose of Courage in teaching chastity of the heart and the goals of Exodus in advocating programs of reorientation therapy.

I would encourage Catholics with SSA desiring both chastity and freedom from unwanted SSA to seek programs within Exodus to increase their heterosexual potential.

They can, for example, attend specific Exodus groups such as Regeneration in the Baltimore and North Virginia areas, and Desert Streams Ministry on the West Coast, which they will find very helpful in their quest to move toward heterosexual inclinations. Metanoia in Seattle is another Exodus group with which Courage has had good relations.[15] I am sure there are other Exodus groups that I could recommend, if I knew them as well as Regeneration, Desert Streams Ministries, and Metanoia. It should also be pointed out that, from our first general conference in 1989 onward, we have invited speakers from Exodus International to at least seven of our annual conferences. I thought it necessary that Courage leaders and members hear speakers who were both devout Christians and involved in reorientation therapy.

Homosexuals Anonymous

Homosexuals Anonymous (HA) was formed by Colin Cook, and its present director is John J. The group emphasizes that it is both Christian and interdenominational, and many Catholics belong to HA. Their primary purpose is to help people to move out of the condition of homosexuality. At the same time, they are like Courage in that they stress the importance of chastity. Along with Regeneration, HA is closest to Courage in its goals and objectives. Similar to AA in its step program, it is unique in its Christian emphasis, as can be seen in its mission statement: "To bring people to an awareness of the love of God for the fallen, the victory of Christ, which leads to freedom from obsessive-compulsive disorders and the identity of our personhood in Christ that leads to the completing of needs which homosexual behavior inappropriately attempts to complete."[16]

The following statement of the philosophy of HA sums up the nature of this spiritual support group:

> Homosexuals Anonymous, a Christian fellowship, holds the view that homosexual activity is not in harmony with the will of God and that the universal creation norm is heterosexuality. Nevertheless, the great message of righteousness by faith in Christ brings mercy and hope to all people in homosexuality.
>
> Christ, the *Imago Dei* (the Image of God) is the restoration of the creation image, in whom all men and women find their identity by faith. The search for wholeness and heterosexuality within ourselves thus comes to an end. Men and women receive Christ as their image of God in whom is their wholeness and heterosexuality. As a trained faith grasps this awareness, there is a breaking of the power of the homosexual inclination so that freedom from the homosexual drive and activity is a real possibility.
>
> H.A., however, does *not* believe that a change in homosexual inclination is a requirement for acceptance with God or entrance into the fellowship of the Church. Although deliverance from homosexual activity is the call of God, the healing of the homosexual inclination will vary according to growth and is a result of our faith identity *with* Christ rather than as a *way* to it.[17] Nevertheless, H.A. holds that the homosexual inclination may be healed and that all who desire it may realize their inborn, though fallen heterosexuality, thus opening the way to heterosexual marriage and family.[18]

Their position on the healing of homosexuality is thought-provoking: "The basic premise of H.A. is that the root causes of homosexuality are spiritual, intra-psychic and relational...H.A. philosophy maintains that the grace of

God through Christ brings freedom and recovery from the spiritual, psychological, and relational distortions of homosexuality."[19] For those in H. A. the framework of recovery is different from that of secular psychology and psychiatry. Often, the latter tend "to define the person's sexuality in terms of physical and emotional responses, i.e., if you have homosexual desires, you are a 'homosexual.' H.A. does not do so." It believes that "sexuality is determined by a wider set of values, namely, those of the person's relation to God, self, and the world."[20]

"Much secular psychology and psychiatry view homosexuality as a fixed condition, as if 'once a homosexual, always a homosexual.'" Again, H.A. sees it differently because of its wider definition of sexuality: "We see homosexuality as a symptom of a confused identity in relation to God, self, and the world." Likewise, cure or recovery for the secular therapist simply means that desires for persons of the same sex have been changed into desires for persons of the other sex. H.A. sees a wider set of values, i.e., "the ending of anger and resentment toward God and parents, an acceptance of self in relationship to God, and a feeling of safety in a world that, though seemingly alien, is nevertheless under God's control."[21]

At this point H.A. stresses that the changing of one's perceptions, both one's way of thinking and of feeling, will gradually modify one's sexual identity and compulsive drives, "bringing a healing repentance of destructive behavior and introducing more positive attitudes toward the opposite sex, and the possibility of choice."[22]

"A change in sexual feelings is, therefore, gradual and dependent on the above altered perceptions, many of which are ignored by secular psychology and psychiatry."

The latter are often limited in their ability to motivate a client; oftentimes, they encourage the person struggling with homosexuality "to accept himself or herself as 'gay,' or 'lesbian' and learn to live with it." On the other hand, Christian counselors and therapists have the richness of the Gospel message with which to inspire persons with SSA to seek emotional growth in the practice of chastity and the reduction of same-sex attractions. "Secular psychology and psychiatry generally have failed to show us the marvelous resources for emotional growth available to it within the Christian community. H.A. draws heavily upon these resources and the results leave no doubt that people can recover from homosexuality."

SUMMARY

My purpose here has been to show how Protestant, Catholic, Jewish, Mormon, and interdenominational communities agree that homosexual genital acts are seriously immoral in the order of nature and under no circumstances can be justified. But they do more than merely agree on the objective nature of the evil. They endeavor to help persons with SSA to abstain from such actions through various programs which are based upon sound philosophy and psychology. All encourage their members to seek to recover their natural heterosexual inclinations through various forms of therapy. All believe in the power of prayer for chastity and for healing from same-sex attraction.

To be sure, there are diverse emphases. Courage places stress on the power of meditative prayer, leading to interior chastity. It seeks psychologists and psychiatrists familiar with the Catholic faith to help those members of Courage who are striving to come out of the condition of homosexuality. PFOX and Homosexuals Anonymous place greater emphases on forms of reorientation therapy. As a therapist, Richard Cohen makes use of standard therapeutic techniques, his own experience of homosexuality, and prayer in helping others recover their natural heterosexual tendencies. May this chapter lead to further discussion among all the members of PATH and with other groups.

NOTES

¹ Positive Alternatives to Homosexuality (PATH), "Change Is Possible," http://www.pathinfo.org/index2.htm.

² Ibid.

³ Ibid.

⁴ Arthur Goldberg, "Learn More and Read a Greeting from Arthur Goldberg, Co-Director of JONAH," JONAH website, http://www.jonahweb.org/cms/e/index.php?option=content&task=view&id=9. Goldberg is quoting a sicha given in 1986 by Rabbi Menachum Schneerson. An abbreviated version, "Rights or Ills," is on the JONAH website at http://www.jonahweb.org/cms/e/index.php?option=content&task=view&id=100&Itemid=33.

⁵ Ibid.

⁶ JONAH may be contacted at JONAH, Post Office Box 313, Jersey City, New Jersey 07303. Call (201) 433-3444 or visit their website at www.Jonahweb.org.

⁷ See the Evergreen International website, http://www.evergreeninternational.org.

⁸ See the International Healing Foundation, http://www.gaytostraight.org/about.asp.

⁹ Ibid.

¹⁰ NARTH, 16633 Ventura Blvd., Suite 1340, Encino, CA 91436.

¹¹ *NARTH Bulletin*, December 2004, p. 2.

¹² PFOX, P.O. Box 561, Fort Belvoir, VA 22060. (703) 360-2225. Visit their website for more information: http://www.pfox.org.

¹³ Quoted by Regina Briggs, http://www.pfox.org. The (2005) link seems to have been discontinued.

¹⁴ See "Who We Are," Exodus website, http://exodus.to/content/category/6/24/57.

15 Metanoia Ministries, P.O. Box 33039, Seattle, WA 98133.

16 Daniel Roberts, "Freedom from Homosexuality: The Third Option," *Interaction*, Winter 1986, p. 6. Newsletter of the Association for Religious and Value Issues in Counseling.

17 Emphasis mine.

18 HAFS, 2000 Statement of Philosophy, P.O. Box 7881, Reading, PA 19603. Available on their website, http://www.ha-fs.org.

19 Ibid.

20 All citations in this paragraph are from the HAFS Statement of Philosophy.

21 All citations in this paragraph are from HAFS, 2000 Statement on the Healing of Homosexuality.

22 Ibid.

23 Ibid.

CHAPTER 12

Dissenting Catholic Organizations

In the preceding chapter, I reviewed several organizations working with persons with same-sex attraction (SSA) in programs helpful to the individual. These organizations are in basic agreement with the Church's pastoral approach to SSA and that of Courage regarding the disordered nature of homosexual acts and therapeutic programs for members. Courage differs from our allies in that Courage does not offer a therapeutic program to help persons with SSA rediscover their natural heterosexual inclination. We are willing, however, to send individuals to reliable therapists and to groups whose principal purpose is reorientation therapy. As has been stressed previously, the principal purpose of Courage is to teach the virtue of interior chastity.

The Catholic organizations considered in this chapter are not in agreement with Catholic teaching on homosexuality on several key points.

Father, could you provide a description of Dignity, New Ways Ministry, and the National Association of Catholic Diocesan Lesbian and Gay Ministries?

Yes, I will begin with Dignity, whose position I have studied over the years since 1969, when it was founded by an Augustinian priest in the Diocese of San Diego.

Dignity USA

Dignity describes itself as "the nation's foremost organization of gay, lesbian, bisexual, and transgendered Catholics, their families, friends, and supporters across the country. It is an independent organization with members and chapters throughout the country."[1]

Dignity has been active in New York since 1972. Dignity avoided direct confrontation with the authentic teaching of the Catholic Church until July 1987. At the Dignity biennial conference in Miami, the following statement was adopted on July 23, 1987, and adopted unanimously by the New York chapter's board of directors on August 12 of that year. "Dignity reaffirms our Statement of Position and Purpose that states 'We believe that gay men and lesbian women can express their sexuality in a manner that is consonant with Christ's teaching. We believe that all sexuality should be exercised in an ethically responsible and unselfish way.' We are also committed to work for the development of the Church's sexual theology. Therefore, in this capacity, we affirm that gay and lesbian people can express their sexuality physically in a unitive manner that is loving, life giving, and life affirming."[2]

"Therefore, Dignity emphatically disagrees with, and calls for a reexamination of the magisterial teachings on 'homosexual activity' between gay and lesbian people, as presently stated in the American Bishop's letter of 1976, *To Live in Christ Jesus*, and in the 1986 *Letter to the Bishops of the Catholic Church on the Pastoral Care of Homosexual Persons*, issued by Joseph Cardinal Ratzinger and the Congregation for the Doctrine of the Faith (CDF)."[3]

On the Dignity website, one can discover Dignity's stated position and purpose. It repeats the 1987 statement: "We believe that gay, lesbian, bisexual, and transgender persons can express their sexuality in a manner that is consonant with Christ's teaching. We believe that we can express our sexuality physically, in a unitive manner that is loving, life-giving and life-affirming. We believe that all sexuality should be exercised in an ethically responsible and unselfish way."[4] Then Dignity speaks of its responsibilities to the Church: "We work for the development of sexual theology, leading to the reform of its teaching and practices regarding human sexuality, and for the acceptance of gay, lesbian, bisexual and transgender peoples as full and equal members of the one Christ."[5]

Basically, the February 15, 2005 statement repeats the July 23, 1987 statement. Both express disagreement with authentic Catholic teaching by the CDF and propose to change it. Both statements express independence from the teaching authority of the Church.

I believe that many people in Dignity see their opinion as merely a question of sexual rights for people with same-sex attraction. But it is much more serious. To declare homosexual acts as morally good is to deny the meaning of marriage as holy and sacred, and for Catholics a sacrament instituted by Christ. Concerning the sacrament of marriage, the *Catechism of the Catholic Church* says: "The matrimonial covenant, by which a man and a woman establish between themselves a partnership of the whole of life, is by its nature ordered to the good of the spouses and the procreation and education of offspring; this covenant between baptized persons has been raised by Christ the Lord to the dignity of a sacrament."[6]

For a Catholic to hold the position Dignity has taken is to deny revealed truth. True, because of ignorance, such a person may not be a formal heretic. His actions lead to serious sin and are gravely wrong. As a member of Dignity he may be involved in various good works. One may pray that he will come to know the truth about homosexuality.

In its response to the October 1, 1986 statement of the CDF, Dignity speaks of "our experience of alienation between gay Catholics and some other members of the Church, including many leaders."[7]

To overcome this alienation, Dignity proposes to dialogue with the Church on her teachings. Dignity expresses sixteen counsels for bishops and Catholic leaders. The difficulty I find with the counsels is that they exhort the hierarchy to be more open to their suggestions, while Dignity remains adamant in rejecting the teaching of the Church on the disordered nature of homosexual acts.[8] Personally, I have dialogued with Dignity leaders in several cities, but at the end of our conversations, although the meetings ended on a friendly note, nothing changed. No real progress was made.

I have admired Dignity for its work with victims of AIDS. It is one area where the Catholic Church is in agreement with Dignity. The Catholic Church throughout the world has demonstrated great compassion for persons with AIDS in her hospitals and clinics. In New York, Cardinal Cooke Hospital typifies such compassion.

From this commentary on Dignity one can perceive the radical differences between Courage and Dignity. Courage accepts the teaching of the Catholic Church that homosexual acts are always disordered, while Dignity rejects this teaching. The principal purpose of Courage, as a spiritual support group, is to teach the virtue of chastity. The principal goal of Dignity, though, is to promote civil unions and "gay marriage."

New Ways Ministry (NWM)

At the University of Pennsylvania, Father Robert Nugent, then a priest of the Archdiocese of Philadelphia, met a Notre Dame nun, Sister Jeannine Gramick. They founded an organization called New Ways Ministry, which challenged the teaching of the Church on the question of the virtue of chastity for persons with same-sex attraction. What I present now is the response of the Congregation for the Doctrine of the Faith (CDF) to this challenge. It is extremely important for the reader to understand the conclusions and disciplinary measures it took to safeguard Catholic doctrine on homogenital acts.

Before examining the July 1999 decision of the CDF on the status of the leaders of New Ways Ministry, Father Nugent, S.D.S., and Sister Gramick, S.S.N.D., I will summarize the background of this organization.[9] The original research on NWM was done by Father Enrique Rueda, who describes NWM as publishers of pro-homosexual literature, with a Catholic favor, "lobbying for pro-homosexual sympathizers, and generally promoting the movement's ideology. One of the group's most important activities is serving as a center for a very extensive network of homosexual and pro-homosexual activists within the Church."[10]

This description is very accurate, as I know from reading their periodical *Bondings*.[11] Father Nugent views homosexual actions as not objectively wrong but as a deviation from the norm. While not measuring up to the norm, these acts can be tolerated for the overall good of the persons concerned.[12]

Father Nugent also introduces a norm based on relationships, i.e., a norm which finds the value of sexual acts not in generative activity or marital union per se, but in the quality of the relationship thereby established. Logically, from this point of view, one can draw the conclusion that such relationships are good if their quality is good. Once one removes the objective norm of sexual behavior, one reduces the official teaching of the Church to a shambles. It is no longer Church doctrine but merely the opinion of "Vatican officials."[13]

The late archbishop of Washington, James Cardinal Hickey, who had made a careful study of the writings of both Sister Gramick and Father Nugent and had written in 1981 to the bishops in the United States about NWM, went to the Congregation for Religious and Secular Institutes (CRSI), requesting that they be removed from their leadership roles in NWM because their teaching was in direct conflict with the teaching of the Church. Thereupon, the CSRI worked through the superiors of Father Nugent and Sister Gramick, and in 1984 they were removed from their leadership roles in NWM.[14] Thereafter, NWM remained under lay leadership, at least in theory. Both Sister Gramick and Father Nugent, however, continued to write, and their writings led to a confrontation with the CDF during the 1990s, culminating in an official CDF letter issued July 13, 1999. The letter notified Sister Gramick and Father Nugent that "they are permanently prohibited from any pastoral work involving homosexual persons."[15]

Not surprisingly, this document was perceived by most in the secular media as too severe and unduly rigorous. One could have hoped, though, for a better response from the Leadership Conference of Women Religious (LCWR), who, in the name of all its members, vehemently opposed the decision of the CDF. That leaders of Dignity and New Ways Ministry would decry this decision was not unexpected, given their premises. The Church, however, has a right to expect from all Catholics, particularly religious, a religious assent of faith to a decision of the CDF, one which was approved by Pope John Paul II. An article in the Catholic News Service gave undue emphasis to the opinions of Catholic dissenters from the decision of the CDF. In light of this confusing publicity, I find it necessary to detail how the Vatican came to its decision. Unless otherwise stated, all quotations are from the CDF letter of July 13, 1999.[16]

The CDF decision came after eighteen years of dialogue between Church authorities in the United States and in the Vatican on one side, and Father Nugent and Sister Gramick on the other. As already mentioned, between 1981 and 1984, Cardinal Hickey asked them to clarify misleading and ambiguous statements in their writings, and, not satisfied with their responses, he forbade them to continue their activities in the Archdiocese of Washington. At the same time, the Congregation for Institutes of Consecrated Life and Societies of Apostolic Life (CICLSAL) "ordered them to separate themselves totally and completely from 'New Ways Ministry.'"[17]

"Despite this action by the Holy See Father Nugent and Sister Gramick continued their involvement in activities organized by NWM, though removing themselves from leadership positions. They also continued to maintain and promote ambiguous positions on homosexuality and explicitly criticized documents of the Church's Magisterium on this issue."[18]

Because of their writings and activities, the CDF and CICLSAL received complaints and urgent pleas requesting clarification from bishops and others in the United States. It was clear that Father Nugent and Sister Gramick continued to present the teaching of the Church as an opinion, as one option among others, and that their position would change the teaching of the Church in a fundamental way. This led the Holy See to establish a commission, under the presidency of Adam Cardinal Maida, to study and evaluate their public statements and activities and to determine whether they were faithful to Catholic teaching on homosexuality.

After the publication of *Building Bridges*, the investigation of the Commission "focused primarily on this book which summarized their activities and thinking."[19] In 1994 the Commission issued its report, which was communicated to the two authors. When their responses to these findings were received, the Commission formulated its final recommendations and forwarded them to the CICLSAL. While the Commission did not overlook some positive aspects in the apostolate of Father Nugent and Sister Gramick, it "found serious deficiencies in their writings and pastoral activities, which were incompatible with the fullness of Christian morality. The Commission, therefore, recommended disciplinary measures, including the publication of some form of Notification, in order to counteract and repair the harmful confusion caused by the errors and ambiguities in their publications and activities."[20]

Since the problems presented by the two authors were primarily of a doctrinal nature, CICLSAL transferred the entire case to the competence of the CDF in 1995. With the hope that the two authors would be willing to express their assent to Catholic teachings on homosexuality and to correct the errors in their writings, the CDF made another attempt at resolution by asking them to respond unequivocally to certain questions regarding their position on the morality of homosexual acts and on the homosexual inclination. Their responses were not sufficiently clear to dispel the serious ambiguities of their position. "Furthermore, another book which they published in 1995, *Voices of Hope,* had made it clear that there was no change in their opposition to fundamental elements of the Church's teaching."[21]

Sister Gramick and Father Nugent "demonstrated a clear conceptual understanding of the Church's teaching on homosexuality, but refrained from professing any adherence to that teaching. Furthermore, the publication... [of their book] *Voices of Hope* had made it clear that there was no change in their opposition to fundamental elements of the Church's teaching."[22]

Since certain aspects of the teaching of Father Nugent and Sister Gramick were clearly not in agreement with the teaching of the Church, and since these erroneous opinions had been disseminated so widely through their publications and pastoral activities, the bishops of the United States were deeply concerned. So also was the CDF, which decided that the case should be resolved, "according to the procedure outlined in its Regulations for Doctrinal Examination."[23]

In the ordinary session of October 8, 1997, the cardinals and bishops who comprise the Congregation "judged that the statements of Father Nugent and Sister Gramick which had been identified through the above-mentioned procedure of the Regulations for Doctrinal Examination were in fact erroneous and dangerous."[24]

After the Holy Father had ratified the decision of the CDF, the above-mentioned erroneous statements were presented to them, through their respective superiors general. Each was asked to respond to the *contestatio* "personally and independently from the other, to allow them the greatest freedom in expressing their individual positions."[25]

At this point in my narration of this important question, one may wonder why I am following the *Notificatio* so exactly. I will submit my commentary later, but first of all I must present the conscientious procedures of the CDF in respecting the freedom of both Father Nugent and Sister Gramick.

To return to the sequence of events, in February 1998, the two superiors general forwarded their responses to the Congregation. In the ordinary sessions of May 6 and 20, 1998, the members of the Congregation carefully evaluated the responses, after receiving the opinions of bishops in the United States and of experts in moral theology. The members of the Congregation were unanimous in their decision that the responses of the two, "while containing certain positive elements, were unacceptable."[26] In each case Father Nugent and Sister Gramick had tried to justify the publication of their books, and neither had expressed personal adherence to the Church's teaching on homosexuality in sufficiently unequivocal terms. Thus, it was decided that they should be asked to formulate a public declaration, expressing their interior assent to the teaching of the Church on homosexuality, and to acknowledge that the two above-mentioned books contained errors. (This was one more chance for both of them to support Church teaching on homosexuality.)

By August 1998, the two declarations arrived and were examined by the Congregation in the ordinary session of October 21, 1998. Once again, they were not sufficient to resolve the problem associated with their writings and pastoral activities. While expressing her love for the Church, Sister Gramick "simply refused to express any assent whatsoever to the teaching of the Church on homosexuality."[27]

Father Nugent was more responsive, "but not unequivocal in his statement of interior assent to the teaching of the Church."[28] It was decided, therefore, by the Congregation that Father Nugent should be given "yet another opportunity to express unequivocal assent."[29] Accordingly, the Congregation formulated a declaration of assent, and with its letter of December 15, 1998, forwarded it to Father Nugent through his superior general.[30]

The response of Father Nugent on January 25, 1999, however, indicated that this attempt had failed. Father Nugent would not sign the declaration he had received; instead he responded by formulating an alternative which modified the Congregation's declaration on certain important points; for example, he would not state that homosexual acts are intrinsically disordered; and he "added a section which calls into question the definitive and unchangeable nature of Catholic doctrine in this area."[31]

Thus, having made repeated attempts to resolve the problems created by the writings and pastoral activities of the two authors, the "Congregation for the Doctrine of the Faith was obliged to declare for the good of the Catholic faithful that the positions advanced by Sister Jeannine Gramick and Father Robert Nugent regarding the intrinsic evil of homosexual acts and the objective disorder of the homosexual inclination were doctrinally unacceptable because they do not faithfully convey the clear and constant teaching of the Catholic Church in this area. Father Nugent and Sister Gramick have often stated that they seek, in keeping with the Church's teaching, to treat homosexual persons 'with respect, compassion, and sensitivity.'[32] However, the promotion of errors and ambiguities is not consistent with a Christian attitude of true respect and compassion: persons who are struggling with homosexuality no less than any others have a right to receive the authentic teaching of the Church from those who minister to them."[33]

Because the ambiguities and errors of the approach of Father Nugent and Sister Gramick have caused confusion among Catholics, harming the community of the Church, the Congregation decreed "that Sister Jeannine Gramick, S.S.N.D., and Father Robert Nugent, S.D.S, are permanently prohibited from any pastoral work involving homosexual persons and are ineligible, for an undetermined period, for any office in their respective religious communities."[34]

On May 14, 1999, John Paul II approved the *Notificatio* and ordered its publication.

I should like to respond to critics in both the secular and religious press by showing the need for clear terminology in explaining Catholic doctrine on homogenital acts and on the very tendency to such. The term *homogenital* is more precise than *homosexual*, because it refers to genital desires and acts. In the name of the Church, the CDF stated that all homogenital acts are "intrinsically evil." This means that under no circumstances can these acts be morally good. They are always evil.

Father Nugent, however, refused to affirm this truth in the profession of faith submitted to him by the CDF; instead, in the profession which he returned to the CDF, he substituted the words "objectively immoral" for "intrinsically evil." "Objectively immoral" has a different meaning to professional moralists. It states that a certain action, for example, stealing jewelry from your employer, is an act of injustice and is objectively immoral; however, were a poor mother to take some loaves of bread from the doorstep of a wealthy family, it would not be stealing; it would not be unjust, because the right to life of the mother and her children outweighs the rights of the wealthy family to the bread. In other words, taking from another under one set of circumstances is objectively immoral; under another set it can be justified as good. There are theologians who hold that homosexual acts are objectively immoral under one set of circumstances, such as promiscuous activity, but not objectively immoral in the situation of what they term a "faithful, monogamous union" between two people of the same sex. Like Father Nugent, these theologians do not use the term "intrinsically evil," i.e., evil by the very nature of the act, because they do not believe that certain kinds of moral acts are always morally evil.

Since CDF is aware of this teaching of dissenting theologians, it regarded Father Nugent's efforts to write his own profession of faith as unacceptable. The CDF gave both Father Nugent and Sister Gramick every chance to state the Catholic teaching clearly and to make a profession of faith concerning it. While Sister Gramick refused to make the profession of faith submitted to her, Father Nugent tried to change the wording, but succeeded only in producing a watered down version.

The other technical expression used by CDF is "objective disorder." Many people do not understand this term. It refers to the inclination towards homogenital acts. The 1986 *CDF Letter to the Roman Catholic Bishops of the World*, section 3, states that inclinations to same-sex genital acts, while not sinful in themselves, are nonetheless an objective disorder. They are termed such because, if one consents to them, one commits an act which is always evil and under no circumstances good. In this regard, Father Nugent and Sister Gramick have failed to stress the significance of this term, and in this failure they are not alone. The October 1, 1997 statement *Always Our Children*, issued by the USCCB Committee on Marriage and Family did not use the term, and in its revision of July 2, 1998, the term was included as a footnote after the original letter had been corrected by the CDF in significant ways.

Some have attempted to dilute the meaning of the term "objective disorder" by stating that various forms of heterosexual lust—such as adultery and premarital sex—are also objective disorders. But in such acts one must distinguish between the inclination towards the opposite sex and the inclination to same-sex acts. The inclination of man toward woman and woman towards man is natural and ordered toward marriage and procreation. The inclination, however, is abused in acts of adultery and sex outside of marriage; but the inclination remains good in itself, though misdirected. This, again, is not a mere academic question. If, for example, you hold that same-sex attraction is good and natural, you wind up regarding same-sex acts as sometimes morally good.

Father Nugent and other authors object to the CDF's use of precise terms, like "intrinsically evil" and "objective disorder," on the score that such terms are "pastorally insensitive" and offend persons with SSA.

Their objection, however, is without substance. Once one explains the meaning of these terms, one discovers that the reader or listener accepts the explanation. For example, I have explained "intrinsically evil" to mean that the action in itself is always evil and can never be morally good; and I have explained "objective disorder" by showing that there is something wrong with same-sex attraction, that those with SSA are moving toward the wrong kind of persons— persons of one's own sex, when they ought to be moving toward persons of the other sex.[35]

Having carefully studied the *Notificatio* (May 31, 1999) that Father Nugent and Sister Gramick be permanently banned from ministry to persons with homosexual inclinations, and six years later having reviewed the responses of Father Nugent (July 14, 1999) and Sister Gramick (July 23, 1999), I make the following observations. In Father Nugent's response to the above decision he claims that his ministry has always been based "on authentic teachings of the Church and traditional theological and pastoral principles" Yet, as is seen from his July 14th response, he refuses to affirm a teaching found in both the CDF statement of December 29, 1975, *Persona Humana (Declaration on Certain Problems Concerning Sexual Ethics)*, section 8, and in the October 1, 1986 *Letter to the Bishops of the Catholic Church on the Pastoral Care of Homosexual Persons*, section 3. In the 1975 statement of CDF one reads: "Sexual relations between persons of the same-sex are necessarily and essentially disordered according to the objective moral order. Sacred Scripture condemns them as gravely depraved, and even portrays them as the tragic consequence of rejecting God...But it does show that homosexual acts are intrinsically disordered and may never be approved in any way whatever."[36]

In *PCHP*, the CDF defines "objective disorder" as a more or less strong tendency ordered toward an intrinsic moral evil, and thus the inclination itself must be seen as an "objective disorder." The inclination, however, is not sinful in itself.[37]

Since Father Nugent does not affirm that the inclination to same-sex acts is an objective disorder or that homogenital acts are disordered, he is not in agreement with the authentic teaching of the Church.

Sister Gramick responded to the CDF decision by claiming that the whole process of investigation was unfair. She continues to hold that the CDF had no right to request her to give interior assent to the teaching that homogenital acts are intrinsically evil and that the inclination was an objective disorder. On the contrary, the CDF sees an important link between interior belief and public statements by anyone in the ministry of the Church. If one does not believe the authentic teaching of the Church to be true, and the documents I cited are authentic teaching, how can one persuade others to believe them? Again, the teaching of the Church on homosexuality is an integral part of her teaching on marriage and human sexuality in general. They are parts of her doctrinal teaching on marriage. Those who vehemently denounced the *Notificatio* of the CDF need to study the record of the investigation, as the CDF has recorded it faithfully. It is a matter in which we place our trust in the competence and integrity of the CDF and in the judgment of our Holy Father, Pope John Paul II, who approved the decision. I have debated with both Father Nugent and Sister Gramick for at least twenty-five years. While respecting them I do not accept their positions.

Benefits of the CDF's Decision

The first benefit was bestowed upon all Catholics with same-sex attraction. They now see beyond a shadow of a doubt that all homogenital acts are "intrinsically evil" and that this teaching requires of us interior assent, the assent of hearts and minds. The second benefit is shared by all Courage members, since it clears the theological air about the morality of homogenital acts and about the homosexual condition itself. Members of Courage and Encourage may regard the CDF decision as an affirmation of Courage, which has been granted the approval of the Pontifical Council for the Family. As already noted, speaking on behalf of the Holy See, Cardinal Lopez Trujillo said: "This Pontifical Council for the Family supports the organization called Courage which was founded by Father John Harvey, OSFS, for helping homosexual persons to live in accordance with the laws of God and the teaching of His Church" (7 July-1994-Prot. N216/93).

The third benefit leads to greater security and greater trust by reducing tension and giving to the faithful a higher level of security in the practice of their faith. The CDF has quieted the complaints that the Holy See is doing nothing to dispel the confusion of many who have come to believe that the judgments of their individual conscience take priority over the certain teaching of the Catholic Church.

National Association of Catholic Diocesan Lesbian and Gay Ministries (NACDLGM)

Note: *While NACDLGM does not dissent from Church teaching on same-sex attraction as explicitly as do the two organizations mentioned previously in this chapter, its leaders are silent on promoting chastity among those with SSA and at least tacitly approve the homosexual lifestyle.*

The National Association of Catholic Diocesan Lesbian and Gay Ministries began in Oakland under the leadership of Father James Schexnayder in 1994. As you read my description of this organization, you will realize that it is very difficult to know what they really believe. They claim to be with the Church, but they do not state their views on the necessity of chastity for persons with same-sex attraction.

At a July 1994 meeting in Chicago, twenty-eight laity, clergy, and religious from thirteen dioceses gathered to discuss diocesan ministries to gay and lesbian Catholics and their families. The group acknowledged that lesbian and gay Catholics, and those who minister to them, face unjust discrimination from some Roman Catholics; they agreed that a voluntary network of people could set up supportive ministries for gay and lesbian people. In 1995, at a second conference in Seattle, the principal purposes of the association were stated, as found in the bylaws: a) to foster ministry with lesbian and gay Catholics, their families and friends; b) to serve as a network of communication among diocesan leaders regarding gay and lesbian ministry; c) to provide educational resources and models of ministry existing in various areas; d) to encourage the participation of lesbian and gay Catholics within the Church; and e) to communicate where appropriate with national Catholic organizations, especially the United States Conference of Catholic Bishops (USCCB).[38]

In March 1999, the board of directors composed a mission statement which urged those in ministry to reflect on Sacred Scripture, Church teaching, and pastoral practice; to study the social and physical sciences; and to listen and ponder the lived experience of lesbian and gay persons and their families. The mission statement affirms the human dignity and rights of lesbian and gay persons, stating that all who are baptized are called to full participation in the life and mission of the Church.[39]

From the above mission statement I went through copies of the association's quarterly publication *Reclaim* to learn more about the pastoral activities of the national association. In the May 2003 issue of *Reclaim,* I came across Father James Graham's review of *This Remarkable Gift—Being Gay and Lesbian,* by Father Maurice Shinnick. In his review Father Graham praises Shinnick's work as "a remarkable book."[40] Graham states that Shinnick "firmly plants himself and his work on the bedrock of Church teaching and practice."[41] Having read Shinnick's book in 1998, I found that Shinnick was opposing the teaching of the Church on homosexual inclinations and acts. Father Shinnick stated that the Church holds that the homosexual *inclination* is an objective disorder because it teaches that homosexual *acts* are "intrinsically disordered," that is to say, by their very nature, disordered. If the acts are disordered, then the inclination to the acts also has to be an objective disorder. This is authentic Church teaching, which Father Shinnick does not accept.[42] On the contrary, he holds that the homosexual inclination is natural and good and it follows that homosexual acts become natural and good.

Recently, however, Father Shinnick has completely changed his position on the issue of homosexual activity. He addresses his remarks to the CDF:

> In writing *This Remarkable Gift* it was never my intention to harm the Church or to scandalize the faithful. Where that happened I express my profound regret and offer a sincere apology. My life as a priest is given to the service of the Church...It has long been a pastoral concern of mine that so many homosexual men and women felt estranged from the Church they love because of their sexuality...There is in the Magisterium of the Church a rich reflection on the teaching on the homosexuality and of pastoral concern for homosexual people...I accept with full submission of heart and mind the authoritative teaching of the Church on homosexuality.[43]

As I read further in *Reclaim* issues,[44] I discerned that the National Association of Catholic Diocesan Lesbian and Gay Ministries was deeply concerned with discrimination against gay and lesbian persons. I resonate with this concern in fifty years of ministry with persons with SSA. In Courage, I have counseled individuals in regard to their rights as persons, particularly concerning privacy rights. But in the five issues of *Reclaim* I perused I found no clear explanation of the virtue of chastity as it is stated in the *Catechism of the Catholic Church*.[45] Chastity is a universal obligation, binding in every condition of life. Peace and justice concerns are important, but so also is the virtue of chastity in the sense taught in the *Catechism*. In section 2357, it is stated: "Basing itself on Sacred Scripture, which presents homosexual acts as acts of grave depravity, tradition has always declared that 'homosexual acts are intrinsically disordered.' They are contrary to the natural law. They close the sexual act to the gift of life. They do not proceed from a genuine affective and sexual complementarity. Under no circumstances can they be approved."

Father, are there common characteristics of all three organizations discussed in this chapter?

The virtue of chastity is necessary for members of any support group designed to help persons with same-sex attraction. None of the three groups discussed in this chapter, however, accept the basic moral teaching of the Catholic Church. Dignity, in one of its general meetings, stated that persons with same-sex attraction have a right to homogenital acts. When pinned down by the Congregation for the Doctrine of the Faith to accept a a creed (a declaration of assent) proposed by CDF, Sister Gramick of NWM refused to do so, while Father Nugent tried to change the wording of the creedal statement. The CDF, in light of the refusal of Father Nugent and Sister Gramick to sign the statement of faith proposed to them, asked them to no longer speak on the issue of homosexual acts. As I have previously mentioned, NACDLGM has yet to affirm the teaching on chastity as it is found in the *Catechism of the Catholic Church*. Thus, all three groups evade the question of chastity for persons with SSA.

Summary

In this chapter, I have described organizations claiming to be Catholic which, however, are not in agreement with Catholic teaching. Dignity is clear in its opposition to the teaching of the Congregation for the Doctrine of the Faith, because it holds that same-sex couples who are faithful to each other should be allowed to engage in some form of sexual intercourse. The CDF teaches that such acts are "intrinsically disordered," i.e., immoral by their very nature. Dignity also promotes same-sex "marriages" in opposition to the position of the Church as stated in the June 3, 2003 document, which holds that such unions in no way fulfill the divine meaning of marriage as the union of one man and one woman.

As explained in the previous pages, New Ways Ministry opposes the teaching of the Church in several ways: 1) it destroys the objective norm of human sexuality, i.e., acts of intercourse between man and woman are morally good only within matrimony. Nugent holds that the morality of such acts depends upon the quality of the relationships; in this situation there is no objective norm; 2) Nugent calls into doubt the competency of the CDF to teach with authority on matters of sexual morality; 3) he refuses to accept the teaching of the same Congregation on the definition of homosexual inclinations as an objective disorder. The CDF says that the inclination, while not sinful in itself, can lead one to an intrinsically disordered act.

The National Association of Catholic Diocesan Lesbian and Gay Ministries is very similar to both Dignity and New Ways Ministries in that it does not affirm Church teaching that the inclination to same-sex genital acts is an objective disorder. In all three groups, moreover, one does not find emphasis on the virtue of chastity, as it is understood in the *Catechism of the Catholic Church*. Again, in their arguments, all three groups place greater emphasis on the "lived experience" of persons with same-sex attraction than on natural moral law and and Holy Scripture. In short, the tenets of all three depart significantly from the authentic teaching of the Catholic Church.

NOTES

1 *Dignity Calendar of NY*, vol. 13, no. 9. This issue contains the history of the dissent of Dignity from the authentic teaching of the Church.

2 Ibid. See also the Dignity website at http://www.dignityusa.org/purpose.html.

3 See note above. See also the proceedings of DignityUSA's Eighth Biennial Convention (July 23-26, 1987) on the Dignity website at http://www.dignityusa.org/archives/1980s.html.

4 Dignity website, http://www.dignityusa.org.

5 Ibid.

6 *CCC*, no. 1601-05.

7 *Letter on Pastoral Care of Gay and Lesbian Persons*, Dignity USA's response to the Vatican's *Letter to the Bishops of the Catholic Church on the Pastoral Care of Homosexual Persons* of October 1986 (July 1987), Dignity website, http://www.dignityusa.org/1986doctrine/pastoral-r.html.

8 Ibid.

9 Harvey, *The Homosexual Person*, pp. 171-74.

10 Enrique Rueda, *The Homosexual Network* (Greenwich, CT: Devin-Adair, 1982), p.353, quoted in John Harvey, *The Homosexual Person*, p. 171.

11 *Bondings*, vol. 25, no. 2 (Fall-Winter, 2005). A publication of New Ways Ministry, 4012 29th St., Mt. Rainier, MD 20712.

12 Harvey, *The Homosexual Person*, p. 171.

13 Ibid., p. 172.

14 Ibid., p. 173.

15 CDF, July 13, 1999. The full title of the letter is *Notification of the Congregation for the Doctrine of the Faith*, May 31, 1999. See also CDF, *Agendi ratio in Doctrinarum examine*, art.23-27, AAS 89 (1997).

16 Harvey, *Courage Newsletter*, Fall 1999.

17 *Notificatio*, p. 1, states that Nugent and Gramick were not to exercise any apostolate without faithfully presenting the Church's teaching about the intrinsic evil of homosexual acts.

18 Ibid.

19 Ibid.

20 Ibid., pp. 1-2.

21 Ibid., p. 2.

22 Ibid.

23 Ibid., p. 2, ch. 4 of the Regulations.

24 Ibid.

25 Ibid.

26 Ibid.

27 Ibid.

28 Ibid.

29 Ibid.

30 Ibid., p. 3.

31 Ibid.

32 *CCC*, no. 2358.

33 *Notificatio*.

34 Ibid.

35 John Harvey, "The Director's Corner," *Courage Newsletter*, 99:4.

36 CDF, *Persona Humana*, no. 8, in *Vatican Council II: More Post Conciliar Documents*, ed. Austin Flannery (Grand Rapids, MI: W. B. Eerdmans, 1982). Also available on the website of EWTN, http://www.ewtn.com/library/curia/cdfcertn.htm.

37 *On th Pastoral Care of Homosexual Persons* (1986), no. 3.

38 http://www.nacdlgm.org/nac_bylaws.html.

39 Ibid.

40 "A Remarkable Book," *Reclaim*, vol. 8, no. 3, pp. 1-2. Father Shinnick's book was published by Allen and Unwin, St. Leonards, Australia, in 1997. After stating the core of Catholic teaching in section three, he argues against it on pp. 2, 4-7.

41 http://www.nacdlgm.org/history.htm.

42 *On the Pastoral Care of the Homosexual Persons*, no. 3.

43 Maurice Shinnick, "For the Congregation for the Doctrine of the Faith," *Australasian Catholic Record* 82, no. 1 (January 2005): pp. 83-85.

44 *Reclaim* issues for February and August 2003; and for February, May, and August 2004.

45 CCC, no. 2337; nos. 2338-2350 are also concerning chastity.

CHAPTER 13

An Encourage Story

Father, in addition to what you have said already, is there anything else that helps parents who contact you in distress about a son or daughter in the homosexual lifestyle?

Yes. Often I put them in contact with the international leaders of Encourage, Robert and Susan Cavera. They are a great source of help to such parents. I include here a piece they have written about Encourage. They tell their personal story but also share practical suggestions for starting and leading Encourage groups.

AN ENCOURAGE STORY
by Robert and Susan Cavera

Devastated is, perhaps, the best word to describe our emotional and mental state after we learned that our youngest son had first questioned his same-sex attraction and later embraced the behavior. We were grief stricken, angry, hurt, ashamed, heartbroken, and frustrated. How could this have happened to him? To us? What did we do to cause this? Where did this come from? How can we "fix" it? Where do we go for help? These feelings and questions became part of our daily routine. Our deepest concern and fear was for his physical, emotional, and spiritual well-being, and it remains so today. Even as we write this, looking over some of the old materials from workshops we have given, and talking about these first months and years, the old pain comes flooding back.

This all happened about fifteen years ago, and since then we have learned a lot from a number of sources. We learned that while the origin of our son's same-sex attraction is complex and multifaceted, it is not something he chose. We also know that unresolved hurts from his childhood must be healed and needs for love and acceptance need to be met. Unwanted same-sex attraction forced him into leading a double life. He was trying to be the good Catholic boy his mom and dad wanted him to be, but he had feelings he did not want and dared not share. We know that through God's grace the healing of these childhood wounds and unmet needs will involve us and other members of the family. We love our son dearly, and we will continue to love him no matter what. Our great regret is that when this all began, we did not know how to share our unconditional love for him. Our thoughts were fixed on our own overwhelming pain and grief. What we failed to recognize was the immense pain our son was in and had been in for many years. In our own pain, we failed to see his pain.

We contacted the pastor of our church and shared our story and our helplessness. He admitted that he had no answers. He did not know anyone in our diocese he could recommend to us. He had very limited experience with this issue. He hoped we would find some answers, and promised to pray for us, which was an encouragement and a blessing. We thank God that he did not say, as we have heard from so very many hurting parents who went to their priests:

"Your son doesn't have a problem; you are the problem. Your son is just being who he is. You need to be more tolerant. The Church will change some day; in the mean time, join PFLAG (Parents and Friends of Lesbians and Gays; a pro-active, pro-gay support group), or join Dignity or attend a New Ways Ministry Conference (two pro-gay groups who identify themselves as Catholic but ignore Church teaching and promote same-sex genital-sexual behavior)."

Thank God our pastor was a faithful priest, and he did not send us into that entangled swamp of false teaching and enabling behavior.

We were led, we believe by God, to share our story and our grief with trusted, godly friends, asking them in confidence to pray for us and for our son. Their prayer support was deeply appreciated, and we felt less alone. But we also had a great need to talk to someone who understood, someone who had experience with this issue. By the grace of God, one dear friend shared a book with us: *Stick a Geranium in Your Hat and Be Happy,* written by Barbara Johnson, director of Spatula Ministry.

We called Barbara, and we were happily surprised that she answered the phone. She offered us consolation and hope, speaking from her experience of having a son in the homosexual lifestyle. We eagerly looked forward to her monthly newsletter, which contained bits of wisdom through humorous anecdotes as well as painful family stories and experiences. Later we contacted Focus on the Family, directed by Dr. James Dobson, and they too were very helpful. They offered counsel and prayers and put us in touch with Exodus and Desert Streams Ministries. We continued to feel, however, the need to find a ministry founded on Catholic spirituality. One day Susan came upon an article about Father John Harvey and the ministry called Courage. At last, we had found a Catholic ministry for persons with same-sex attraction and their families. We called the number provided, and the secretary blessed us with understanding and encouragement. Although she has since retired, we remain in touch with her and she continues to pray for us and for our son. Father Harvey, as it happened, was in the office and spoke directly with Susan. We at once knew that we were "home." Father sent us materials written from a Catholic perspective and put us on the Courage mailing list.

Finally, we were connecting to our Church and to a history of teaching that reflects over two-thousand years of tradition. Coincidentally (another gift from God), Father Harvey was scheduled to speak at a high school about an hour away from us and suggested we meet him. I took a day off from work, and we went to see him. It was such a blessing to meet him, and it is such a blessing to know him. We shared our story, which we thought was unique, but he assured us that he had heard similar stories many times. He encouraged us to pray for our son, to seriously consider establishing a chapter of the Courage and Encourage ministry in our diocese, and to better prepare ourselves by attending the annual Courage conference.

We took the pamphlet explaining Courage and Encourage to our pastor. He read the Five Goals of Courage:

1. To live chaste lives in accordance with Church teaching.

2. To dedicate our entire lives to Christ.

3. To foster a spirit of fellowship with others who struggle.

4. To develop chaste friendships.

5. To live lives that serve as good examples to others.

He was enthusiastic. "This is it," he said. "You have found a genuine Catholic ministry."

Soon the bishop invited Father Harvey to address a gathering of all our diocesan priests, deacons, and religious educators. I was asked to publicly address this august group, but after only a few sentences, I grew too emotional to speak. After this gathering, we thought all we had to do was to sit back and wait for things to happen.

Actually, nothing happened! We waited almost a year and nothing happened. One day, we ran into a priest friend, who supported the idea for the ministry, and he asked us what we were waiting for. We said we were patiently waiting for the wheels of the diocese to engage. He smiled, amused at our naïve understanding. He then spoke directly with the bishop, and with his consent, we attended our first annual Courage conference.

At the conference we were blessed in so many wonderful ways. We met courageous men and women whose daily commitment to prayer, frequent reception of the sacraments, and personal spiritual growth were an inspiration to us. We met grieving parents whose sons or daughters had embraced a lifestyle that, like us, had caused them personal devastation, and we met spouses whose husbands or wives had abandoned their family for the arms of a same-sex lover. We made life-long friendships. We found ourselves speaking with men and women in ways we wished we could share with our son, and we suspect that they spoke to us in heartfelt ways that they longed to share with their own parents and families. Finally, at this conference and at every conference since, we have met courageous men and women who have embraced the cross. They were like Mary, the Mother of our Lord, who stood at the foot of the cross believing that God's promises would be fulfilled. They, like her, had never abandoned hope, nor should we.

We returned home and shared with our pastor the wonderful gift of the Courage conference, and he took us to see the bishop. Our pastor had the bishop's complete confidence, and the bishop was eager to start a ministry to persons with same-sex attraction and to their families and friends. He gave us his blessing and a modest budget. We drafted a letter to send, under his signature, to all the priests of the diocese. He organized a dinner meeting and invited priests to attend an informational session, where a priest prominent in the Courage ministry would speak to them—priest to priest. A few came and we began the ministry. Over a period of time, we were able to put a separate phone line into the parish office of our pastor, who was appointed the group's chaplain/ spiritual advisor by the bishop. With the help of a wonderful deacon and a willing secretary, we prepared materials that would complement the Courage and Encourage brochure to be sent to anyone seeking information or help. We wrote to all the priests and religious educators informing them of our existence, including the Courage informational pamphlet, and we established a regular monthly meeting schedule. This may all sound wonderful, but it didn't come without a struggle.

The presence of Courage and Encourage caused division with some diocesan employees and priests, who misunderstood or were ignorant of the goals of Courage, or who did not embrace the Catholic Church's teaching on homosexuality as stated in the *Catechism*, and had an "alternative" view for the "alternative lifestyle." This caused some serious problems at first. Frankly, we were not prepared for the opposition. In the midst of the difficulties we continued to search for healing for ourselves and for others. As we struggled to work our way through the grief process, we realized that we were becoming stronger as we deepened our faith and trust in the Lord and reached out to others who were hurting. As a result, the Lord revealed to us how to move "from pain to peace." We have come to call these insights gained along the way the Four P's: Pray, Prepare, Persevere, and Proclaim.

1. **Pray**. Seek to deepen your relationship with our Lord Jesus Christ and His Blessed Mother, and surrender your loved one to the loving hand of God at the foot of the cross. Make use of the many opportunities the Catholic tradition offers to grow in holiness. If at all possible, pray daily with a supportive person, for example, your spouse, a dear friend, or a trusted family member. Pray that all your children will embrace the Church's teaching on chastity, life, and marriage.

2. **Prepare**. Educate yourselves about the truth concerning homosexuality. (A select annotated bibliography follows this chapter.) Attend the annual Courage conference.

3. **Persevere**. Persevere in prayer. Persevere in the face of disappointments and obstacles. Most importantly, persevere in maintaining good communication and contact with the loved one with same-sex attraction. This is vital.

We have no influence if we are not speaking to the people we love. And persevere in patient hope, waiting for the opportunity to share God's healing truth in love and with encouragement. Persevere also in taking care of yourself. This cannot become the only focus of your life; look for opportunities to have fun, such as to watch a funny movie or spend a weekend away. Be aware that reading about homosexuality can be emotionally upsetting, especially the pro-gay-rights material.

4. **Proclaim the truth**. Go to your pastor and share Courage and Encourage with him. Seek to become a resource. Discern how and when to share with family members, for example, those who may challenge the Church's position regarding same-sex attraction and behavior. Be ready to proclaim the truth in love. We would also suggest that you ask the Lord for discernment as to how and when to publicly share about the Courage and Encourage ministry and about your own testimony as it relates to the ministry. Before you share publicly, ask permission from your loved one with same-sex attraction. Should he or she object, do not publicly proclaim your involvement. Our son is aware of our activity with Encourage and has given us his permission to be public. Proper language is very important. Designating someone by the label "gay," "lesbian," "transgendered," or "bisexual" reduces that person to his or her sexual attractions or sexual behaviors. The Church teaches that each human being is a child of God, and by grace heir to eternal life.

Our Encourage Group

Our diocesan Encourage group is a spiritual support group that meets once a month on Sunday afternoon from 2:30 to 4:00 p.m. Ten days before each meeting we prepare and mail out several hundred letters to persons who have expressed an interest in being on our mailing list. With this letter we also send an informational piece; for example, we recently sent the article "How America Went Gay," by Charles W. Socarides, M.D. When we first started meeting nine or ten years ago, we mailed ten or fifteen letters, and for several months the only attendees at the meeting were the two of us. Our chaplain encouraged us: "I don't care if not a soul shows up for the entire year; I want you to meet at the same time and in the same place." So we did, and God blessed us with inquirers who came hurting and looking for help.

Every meeting has an agenda that includes introductions and opening prayers, followed by personal sharing. We always have ready a "focus of personal growth" prepared beforehand, for example, "The Twelve-Step Review," by Fr. Emmerich Vogt, O.P. But the primary focus is on support for those who are hurting, which takes precedence over our prepared input. We close with a sharing of prayer needs for the month and a final prayer. Ordinarily we have ten to fourteen participants. Some are regulars and have been with us from the beginning. They are very important to us, and we have come to rely on their wise counsel and strong faith. Others come two or three times, and then we don't see them again. God seems to send to each meeting someone new, someone who needs our support. We pray for each other, support each other, sometimes maintain phone contact with each other, and we attempt to deepen our relationship and trust in the Lord.

Because the diocese gives us a small annual budget, we are able to maintain an office. We have also received donations from unexpected sources. One couple drove about ninety miles to our meeting, tearfully shared their story, prayed with us, made a surprise sizeable cash donation, and we never saw them again. We think they were angels. One parish in the diocese gives us an annual donation from their tithe. These gifts are essential to our survival. We have a phone in a local parish office, and the secretary is trained to answer the phone, forward messages, and mail out inquiry packets. The budget and donations allow us to pay the postage for monthly announcements; make annual mailings to all priests, directors of religious education, deacons, and parish administrators; buy books, CDs, and DVDs for the small library we maintain; reimburse the parish for the secretary's time and materials used; pay the phone bill; and help with meeting expenses for Courage and Encourage in the diocese. We are listed as an official diocesan ministry, and this is advantageous when we need to publicize the ministry in official diocesan publications.

We are often asked how we were able to secure, though small, an annual budget from the diocese. The most accurate answer is through the grace of God. We had, from the beginning, purposed not to bypass in any way the structured authority of the Church.

Starting Courage and Encourage in Your Diocese

Two elements are essential in starting a Courage and/or Encourage group in your diocese: a) a faithful priest who will be in it for the long haul, and b) the approval of your bishop. We believe God honors that structure, and we believe that our yielding to the authority God has given us allows us the freedom to grow. We, therefore, would recommend the following:

1. Locate a priest who supports the Church's teachings on SSA and who is willing to act as your chaplain—a priest who, even if he is not able to attend meetings regularly, will be available for counsel and spiritual direction. Hopefully, he also has some influence with the bishop and is willing to intercede on your behalf.

2. Send a packet of information to the bishop, the diocesan chancellor, and any others you can think of, and request a meeting with the bishop. We suggest sending the pamphlets about Courage/Encourage and *Hope and Homosexuality.* by the Catholic Medical Association. Don't overwhelm them with information.

3. Come to the meeting with the packet of information (in case it was misplaced) and some additional information. Have a plan for the ministry. Know the location of the meetings, the frequency, the priest or deacon who will act as chaplain (hopefully he is sitting there with you), an outline of meeting activities, and an assurance that you will operate under the authority of the Bishop.

4. Ask to be recognized as an official diocesan ministry and to be added to the website and other documents.

5. Ask permission to prepare a letter for the bishop's signature that announces Courage and Encourage as the only official diocesan ministry to persons with same-sex attraction and to their families and friends. Send the letter to all priests, deacons, and religious educators in the diocese, as well as to diocesan agencies such as Social Services, Peace and Justice, and Catholic Charities. Include an informational packet with a local address and phone number attached, or include a local Courage/Encourage business card.

6. Ask for a small yearly budget (three to five thousand dollars) to cover the cost of mailings, phone, and materials.

7. Write to the bulletin editor in each parish, providing an announcement to be included in the parish bulletin. Be sure to use correct language. You will need to do this at least three or four times a year. Most of our inquiries come as a result of someone reading a bulletin announcement.

8. Meet with the diocesan director of communications and ask that information about the ministry be included in the regular communiques to the parishes. You will also need the mailing lists of priests, deacons, and directors of religious education.

9. Plan an annual mailing to all priests, deacons, and parish administrators to keep them updated on the Courage and Encourage ministry. Include a small informational packet.

10. If your diocese sponsors general conferences, ask to be included as a workshop presenter and to have an informational table.

Pray about your involvement in this ministry. and as you pray for your loved one with same-sex attraction, pray for your role in his or her life and in the life of the Church. We see a great need for the ministry of Courage and Encourage in more dioceses, and we pray that some of you will develop the ministry where you live.

SELECT ANNOTATED BIBLIOGRAPHY

Annotations by Fr. James Knapp, S.J.

Augustine. *Confessions.* Translated by F. J. Sheed. New York: Sheed and Ward, 1943. Rev. ed., New York: Hackett Publishing, 1993.

Birch, Paul James. "Pornography Use: Consequences and Cures." *Resources for Overcoming Inappropriate Internet Use: Overcoming Addiction to Internet Pornography.* http://overcome.byu.edu/articles/birch.asp.

Catholic Medical Association. *Homosexuality and Hope.* November 2000. http://www.cathmed.org/publications/homosexualityarticle.htm.

Deals with questions about the origin and causes of homosexual attraction in men and women, evidence for and against a genetic cause or predisposition, and whether it is possible or advisable to pursue a therapeutic program for "change" from same-sex attraction to heterosexual attraction.

Demarco, Donald. "Pornography: Formula for Despair." *Catholic Education Resource Center.* http://www.catholiceducation.org/articles/sexuality/se0046.html.

Finnis, John. "Law, Morality, and 'Sexual Orientation.'" *Notre Dame Law Review* 69 (1994): 1049-76.

A highly respected moral theologian discusses the moral issues related to same-sex attraction and how they emerge in the public square.

Fitzgibbons, Richard. "The Origins and Healing of Homosexual Attractions and Behaviors." In *The Truth about Homosexuality*, by John F. Harvey, O.S.F.S., 307-43. San Francisco: Ignatius, 1996.

The author's conclusions on the emotional causes of homosexual attraction and behavior are based on more than twenty years of work with hundreds of men and women who have struggled with same-sex attraction.

Flanagan, Michael. "The Medical Abnormality of Homosexuality." *Linacre Quarterly* (August 2003): 232-49.

Flanagan, who is a physician, catalogues the various health risks involved in acts associated with an active "gay lifestyle." HIV/AIDS is only one of many problems.

Francis de Sales. *Introduction to the Devout Life*. Translated by John K. Ryan. New York: Harper and Row, 1966. Reprint, New York: Image, Doubleday, 1989.

Gagnon, Robert A. J. *The Bible and Homosexual Practice*. Nashville: Abingdon Press, 2001.

Grace, Rebecca. "When Dad Falls: A Family's Ordeal with Pornography." AgapePress, September 8, 2004. http://headlines.agapepress.org/archive/9/afa/82004c.asp.

Grisez, Germain. *The Way of the Lord Jesus*. Vol. 2, *Living a Christian Life*. Quincy, IL: Franciscan Press, 1993, 644-56.

Along with his first volume, which is concerned with fundamental moral theology, this volume deals with nearly every pressing moral problem of our time. The text is clear and amply supported with notes and references. Highly recommended.

Groeschel, Benedict, C.F.R. *The Courage to Be Chaste.* New York: Paulist, 1988.

A brief book on human sexuality from a spiritual and psychological point of view. Very important for persons dealing with same-sex attraction. Dedicated to the men and women of Courage.

Harvey, John F., O.S.F.S. *The Homosexual Person: New Thinking in Pastoral Care.* San Francisco: Ignatius, 1987.

Father Harvey's first comprehensive treatment of homosexuality. A groundbreaking work with an enduring contribution and popularity.

_____. "The Pastoral Problem of Masturbation." Courager.net. http://www.couragerc.net/PIPMasturbation.html/.

Advice for confessors and counselors.

_____. "Source of Same-Sex Attractions in Children: Parenting and Social Influences: Father John Harvey Distinguishes the Difference: Interview with Father John Harvey." ZENIT News Agency, January 24, 2004. http://www.zenit.org/article-17451?l=english/.

_____. *The Truth about Homosexuality: The Cry of the Faithful.* San Francisco: Ignatius, 1996.

An expansion of the insights of *The Homosexual Person,* with some contributions by other authors. A deeper treatment of psychological issues and an expanded treatment on living a lifestyle faithful to the Church's teaching. Includes a separate chapter on homosexual attraction in women. Also addresses contemporary issues like homosexual unions.

Harvey, John F., O.S.F.S., and Gerard V. Bradley, eds. *Same-Sex Attraction: A Parents' Guide*. South Bend, IN: St. Augustine's Press, 2003.

Pastorally sensitive, theologically orthodox, scientifically accurate. Anthology of articles by a number of highly respected experts in a variety of fields.

John Paul II. *Familaris Consortio (The Role of the Christian Family in the Modern World)*. Boston: Pauline Books and Media, 1981.

Contemporaneous with his "theology of the body" teachings at weekly audiences, Pope John Paul II's theology of marriage and human sexuality is found here.

_____. *Theology of the Body: Human Love in the Divine Plan*. Boston: Pauline Books and Media, 1997.

Moberly, Elizabeth. *Homosexuality: A New Christian Ethic*. Cambridge, England: James Clarke, 1983.

Cogently discusses the issues involved in same-sex attraction from spiritual, psychological, and moral perspectives.

Morrison, David. *Beyond Gay*. Huntington, IN: Our Sunday Visitor Press, 1999. One man's story of coming out of the gay lifestyle and finding support through Courage and the Catholic faith.

Van den Aardweg, Gerard J. M. *The Battle for Normality*. San Francisco: Ignatius, 1997.

Comprehensive approach to the origins of the homosexual condition by a psychiatrist who has much experience in the field.

West, Christopher. *The Theology of the Body Explained*. Boston: Pauline Books, 2003.

Published as a companion volume, and commentary on, John Paul II's *Theology of the Body*.

INDEX

ABOUT THE AUTHOR

Father John F. Harvey, O.S.F.S., was ordained to the priesthood in 1944. He holds a master's degree in experimental psychology and a doctorate in moral theology from the Catholic University of America, and served as professor of moral theology at De Sales School of Theology for thirty-eight years.

The author of *The Homosexual Person* (Ignatius, 1987), *The Truth About Homosexuality: The Cry of the Faithful* (Ignatius, 1996), and (with Gerard Bradley) *Same-Sex Attraction: A Parents' Guide* (St Augustine Press, 2003), Father Harvey has been giving counsel and guidance to persons with same-sex attraction for more than fifty years.

At the request of Terence Cardinal Cooke, Father Harvey became the first director of the Courage apostolate in 1980 and continues in this post. Meanwhile, Courage has grown from a local New York group to more than a hundred chapters throughout the world.